COOKBOOK

GARY DOWNIE

Illustrated by
Gail Bennett

W.H. ALLEN · LONDON
1985

Abbreviations:

tsp	–	teaspoon
tb	–	tablespoon
oz	–	ounce
lb	–	pound
g	–	gramme
pt	–	pint
fl oz	–	fluid ounce
ml	–	millilitre
dl	–	decilitre

Note:

In the following recipes three sets of weights or measures are given: British, American and metric. British and American dry measures are the same.
These measures are not interchangeable.

Gary Downie is a multi-talented individual: dancer, choreographer and now expert intergalactic cook. He has worked on many shows in London's West End, and his TV credits include *I, Claudius*, *Poldark*, *Nicholas Nickleby*, *Wuthering Heights* and, of course, *Doctor Who*. He is currently working as a Production Manager in the BBC's Drama Department.

Typeset by Phoenix Photosetting, Chatham, Kent
Printed and bound in Great Britain by
Mackays of Chatham Ltd, Kent
for the Publishers, W.H. Allen & Co. PLC
44 Hill Street, London W1X 8LB

ISBN 0 491 03214 5

CONTENTS

ACKNOWLEDGEMENT
The author wishes to thank the many contributors to this book.
All the recipes have been provided by the artistes, staff, writers etc.
of *Doctor Who*.

This book is dedicated to Rita and Peonie, who have helped me and given me encouragement all my life.

SOUPS

Patrick Troughton

The second Doctor

Patrick Troughton, it is true to say, has been one of the most popular Doctors in the series. His characterisation as the clown/hobo is unique. For many years his fans were deprived of seeing him at conventions or hearing him speak publicly, as he was and is a very private, shy and retiring person.

Then in 1983, John Nathan-Turner, the producer of *Doctor Who*, persuaded Patrick to attend the twentieth anniversary *Doctor Who* Celebrations at Longleat House. The fans were more than delighted, as was proved by the standing ovation that Patrick received on his entrance at the gathering. It is because of his confidence in John Nathan-Turner that Patrick attended major US conventions in Chicago in 1983 and 1984 and the *Doctor Who* weekend at the National Film Theatre in London.

I first met Patrick when I was working on a TV series called *Treasure Island* which was being filmed in Corsica, and Patrick was playing a rather unsavoury pirate called Israel Hands. The film unit was waiting in the lobby of the unit hotel at 7.30 am one morning for the coach to take everyone to the location when Patrick appeared in his dirty costume, four weeks' growth of beard and long dishevelled wig, and all of a sudden he was surrounded by a bus tour of young people shouting 'It's Doctor Who!' Patrick was speechless.

As he said, signing autographs, 'It has been ten years since I played the part of the Doctor and they still remember me. That is the power of *Doctor Who*.'

About four years later I once again worked with Patrick. This time the programme was the twice-weekly serial *Angels* in which Patrick's son, Michael, played the part of his son in the show. It was wonderful watching real father and son acting together; being related brought more depth to their roles. Working with Patrick again on the 'The Two Doctors' was a delight. Colin Baker, Nicola Bryant, Frazer Hines and Patrick got on like a house on fire, though the heat in Spain where we filmed in August was sweltering!

Patrick is a kind and considerate person, always ready with a smile and a chat. Here for your amusement is Patrick's dish, which is a filling soup.

Vegetable Soup with Dalek Krotons

Ingredients:

1 small onion
1 turnip
1 carrot
2 potatoes
1 ½ pts/30 oz/9 dls stock (bouillon)
1 oz/28 g butter
1 tb/1 ¼ tb/30 g flour
Salt and pepper
Nutmeg
2 crushed cloves of garlic for the 'Krotons'
2 slices of white bread

Method:

Wash, peel and cut the vegetables into very thin slices (these could also be grated). Melt the butter in a pan, add the vegetables and stir them over the heat for 10 minutes. Make sure not to brown the vegetables. Add the stock or water and simmer for one hour. Remove the scum that appears on the top and season with salt and pepper and nutmeg to taste. Mix the flour and the milk together until it becomes a smooth paste. Then add this to the soup. Boil the soup for 10 minutes.

Dalek Krotons

Dice two slices of white bread. Then melt a knob of butter and a little oil in the frying pan. Crush two cloves of garlic (Dalek) and stir this with the oil and the butter. Fry the diced bread – (Kroton Squares) until golden brown.

Serve piping hot soup topped with the golden brown Dalek Krotons.

Author's Note:

I like this vegetable soup very much. It reminds me of when I used to come home from school in the middle of winter and there to greet me was a piping hot plate of home-made soup.

Rula Lenska

Styles in 'Resurrection of the Daleks'

Rula was born on September 30, 1947. She went to the St Neots School in Hertfordshire and the Ursuline Convent in Westgate-On-Sea. She then trained as a secretary but decided that she would rather become an actress, so she enrolled at the Webber Douglas Academy of Dramatic Art. Her greatest TV success was in the highly successful series *Rock Follies*, but she has made many appearances in other British TV shows including *Dixon of Dock Green*, *The Doctors*, *The Brothers*, *Edward VII*, *Special Branch*, *The Saint*, *Private Schultz*, *Minder*, *Design For Living*, *Watching You*, *To The Manor Born*, *Take A Letter*, *Mr Jones*, *Seven Dials Mystery* and *Battle of the Bands*, and she has appeared on virtually every quiz show on British TV. She also appeared as Styles in *Doctor Who*. Her theatre credits are *Suddenly at Home*, *Flare Path*, *Forget Me Not Lane*, *A Midsummer Night's Dream*, *Secretary Bird*, *Candle in the Wind*, *Abel, Where is your Brother*, and *Mr Fothergill's Murder*. Her movies include *Soft Beds, Hard Battles*, *Alfie Darling*, and *Royal Flash*. Her star sign is Libra and her hobbies are cooking, music, singing, and handiwork. Rula is of Polish descent and so for your pleasure here is her Polish recipe.

Chlodnik (Summer Beetroot Soup)

Ingredients:

1 pt/20 oz/6 dl beef stock (bouillon)
1 cupful of shredded cooked beetroot
1 cupful of raw cucumber cut into thin strips
Fresh beetroot stems cut into 1 inch pieces
Lots of dill (fresh or dry)
1 carton sour cream
1 small carton plain yoghurt
3 hard boiled eggs
Salt and pepper
Sugar to taste

Method:
Cook the beetroot stems and dill in the stock for a few minutes until it begins to boil. Take off the boil and add all the ingredients. When cool, whisk in the sour cream and yoghurt. Place the quartered eggs on four plates and cover them with Chlodnik. This can be served with garlic bread or herb bread.

Author's Note:
High in cholesterol, but very tasty for those hot summer nights and exotic evenings. This dish is a meal in itself, and quite filling. A quick dish to make. I can recommend it.

Jon Pertwee

The third Doctor

Jon Pertwee took over as the Doctor in 1970 and played the part until 1974. His portrayal of the Doctor was very well received by all the fan clubs around the world.

Jon comes from a very theatrical family. His father was Roland Pertwee, the author of many stage dramas. His aunt was an actress, his grandmother was an opera singer, his brother Michael Pertwee a celebrated playwright with many West End credits to his name, and his cousin Bill Pertwee is also a well-known English actor.

Jon Pertwee is and always will be a gadget fiend. For as long as I have known him he has been interested in cars, motorbikes, boats and aeroplanes. You name it, and Jon will try it. His enormous energy and drive stood him in good stead for one of the longest running BBC radio serials called *The Navy Lark* which gave me many hours of pleasure during my childhood. I never dreamt that I would one day not only meet him but also work with him!

I first met Jon when we were both playing in the West End version of *A Funny Thing Happened on the Way to the Forum.* I played one of the Proteans and Jon played a character called Marcus Lycus, the owner of a house of ill repute. The show ran for eighteen months and during those eighteen months I was filled with laughter and joy every night. Jon was very kind to me, offering me invaluable advice on the art of comedy. His stamina is absolutely amazing. He would arrive at the theatre and do the performance of *Forum* after probably having spent all day filming. Then, after the show he would jump into his car and travel hundreds of miles to perform his cabaret act, arriving home in the early hours of the morning. Later that morning the routine would start all over again. In those days Jon also found time to be involved with a scuba diving school and a water skiing school on the island of Ibiza.

Jon Pertwee's other stage credits include *There's a Girl in my Soup*, *The Bedwinner*, and *Irene*. His other work for TV includes a quiz show called *Whodunnit*, and his most famous role after the Doctor is Worzel Gummidge. His screen credits are *The House that Dripped Blood*, in which he appeared with Ingrid Pitt, *One of our Dinosaurs is Missing*, and *The Curious Case of Santa Claus.*

Courgette (Zucchini) Soup

This freezes for 6 months and serves 8 people

Ingredients:

2 large chopped onions
2 oz/¼ cup/225 g butter
2½ lb/1133 g diced courgettes (zucchini)
2 pt/4 cups/1 litre boiling water
4 chicken cubes
¼ tsp/1 g garlic powder
Celery salt
Salt and pepper to taste
½ pt/1 cup/¼ litre cream

Method:

In a large saucepan sautée the onions until they are tender but not browned. Add the diced courgettes, the boiling water and the chicken cubes, the garlic powder, the celery and the salt and pepper. Blend in the food processor or blender until smooth.

Before serving gently heat the soup and add the cream.

Maureen O'Brien

Vicki – Companion to the first Doctor

Maureen O'Brien started her career in the theatre working as an assistant stage manager for the Everyman Theatre in Liverpool. Her first appearance in *Doctor Who* was as the orphan, Vicki, in 'The Rescue' and she left after 'The Myth Makers'. This made a total of nine *Doctor Who* stories. Some of her theatre appearances have been in *The Merchant of Venice* and *The Seagull* and her TV dramas include *The Whiteoaks of Jalna*, *The Lost Boys* and *The Legend of King Arthur*, in which she played the part of the wicked Morgan Le Fey.

Here for you now is Maureen's cold soup, best eaten in Summer.

Vickissoise Soup

Ingredients:

1 lb/453 g leeks (well cleaned)
1 lb/453 g peeled potatoes
2 oz/50 g butter
1 crushed clove of garlic
Salt
Freshly ground black pepper
1½ pt/30 oz/9 dl chicken stock (bouillon)
½ pt/10 oz/3 dl single (light) cream
1 tsp/1¼ tsp/6 ml mint sauce (bottled)
Freshly grated nutmeg
Chopped chives

Method:
Slice the leeks thickly and cut the potatoes into cubes. Process the leeks until they are finely chopped. Remove them from the bowl and do the same with the potatoes. Melt the butter in a large saucepan and add the leeks, potatoes, and garlic. Cook for 5 minutes. Season and stir the stock. Bring to the boil, cover and simmer for 40–45 minutes. Cool slightly then strain the liquid off. Return the vegetables to the processor and process until smooth for about 30 seconds. Add ½ pt (300 ml) of the liquid and process briefly to mix. Pour the soup into a bowl and stir in the remaining liquid. Chill the soup thoroughly and then stir in the cream and mint sauce. Garnish with ground nutmeg and chives before serving.

Author's Note:
This soup has been called the 'Queen of Soups'. I love it and will serve this to most of my friends during the summer. It is essentially a summer soup. The mint sauce adds another dimension to the taste.

Nicholas Courtney

Brigadier Lethbridge-Stewart

Nicholas Courtney is one of the few actors who has appeared with all the Doctors (with the exception of Colin Baker). However, by the time this book is published the situation could have changed. *Stay Tuned*?

The only Doctor he did not appear with as the famous Brigadier was William Hartnell – he played Bret Vyon.

Nick is a popular figure at conventions in the United Kingdom as well as the United States of America. Those who have had the opportunity of meeting Nick at one of the conventions will know that he has the reserve of an English Gentleman, combined with just the right amount of cheeky charm, plus the smattering of a very dry sense of humour.

Nicholas Courtney and I are great friends. Whenever I fly to the US for a convention, Nick's enormous talent as a raconteur makes the sometimes tortuous journey fly by. I am pleased to say that he has been busy as an actor in theatre and films, as well as finding time to fit in the occasional appearance as the 'Brig'! Nick will be cropping up again later in this book, but for the time being here is Nicholas Courtney's Borscht.

Borscht

Ingredients:

¼ small white cabbage
2 large carrots
2 turnips (in season)
2–3 potatoes (best average size and not too large)
1 large beetroot (or 2 small beetroots)
Beef stock (bouillon)
Salt to taste
1 large carton of sour cream

Method:

1) Shred the cabbage and bring to the boil; then simmer slowly in salted water for about 2 hours.
2) Shred the carrots and the turnips and add them to the simmering cabbage and continue to simmer slowly for 30 minutes.
3) Shred the potatoes and add them to the simmering vegetables with the beef stock (or the beef cubes). Continue to simmer very gently.
4) Shred and add the beetroot at the last moment. Heat the soup to just below boiling point, but do not boil.

Then serve sour cream at the table for everyone to help themselves.

Author's Note:

It is advisable to cook the cabbage the day before. When you get the cabbage to boiling point on the next day, add the other vegetables. Borscht is a lovely soup on its own but simply delicious when sour cream is added, as Nick suggests. Very rich in taste.

Nerys Hughes

Todd in 'Kinda'

Nerys Hughes was born on November 8, 1941 in Rhyl in Wales and was educated at Howells School, Denbigh. She originally trained as a teacher at the Rose Bruford Training College but soon made a name for herself on TV when she appeared in a series called *The Liver Birds* which ran for ten years. She then went on to appear on TV in *The Merchant of Venice*, *High Summer Seasons*, *Diary of a Young Man*, *How Green Was my Valley* (I became friendly with Nerys while she was making this show), *Jackanory*, *Play Away*, *Third Time Lucky*, and of course as Todd in *Doctor Who*.

She is married to BBC TV Film Cameraman, Patrick Turley, and has a son and a daughter. Her star sign is Scorpio and her hobbies are playing with the children and gardening. Nerys is one of the most sincere people that I know. If she says she will do something then she will. She is very kind-hearted and helpful.

Nerys's recipe is a traditional Welsh dish, and is called 'Kinda Soup', but it is really Welsh Leek Soup. I trust that you will find it delicious.

Nerys's 'Kinda' Soup

Ingredients:

4 medium sized leeks (sliced and thoroughly washed)
1 small onion (peeled and sliced)
3 medium sized potatoes (peeled and sliced)
1 oz/28 g butter
2 pt/40 oz/12 dl stock (bouillon)
Salt and pepper
3 tbs/3¾ tbs/57 ml cream
Bunch of parsley

Method:

Lightly fry the vegetables in the butter for about 5 minutes, until they are soft but not coloured. Add the stock. Cover and simmer for 45 minutes until the vegetables are cooked.

Purée the vegetables in a blender until smooth and then return to the pan. Reheat and season with the salt and pepper. Then stir in the cream just before serving. Scatter sprigs of fresh parsley on top of the soup.

Author's Note:

This soup is delicious accompanied with chunks of whole grain bread, with lots of butter or margarine. It tastes even better if the bread is still warm.

John Nathan-Turner

Producer – Doctor Who

John Nathan-Turner was born on August 12 in nineteen-hundred-and-frozen-to-death in the Midlands. He was educated at King Edward's School, Aston, and Longdon Hall, Staffordshire. John turned down a place at Hull University to read German in favour of a theatrical career.

After a short spell as Stage Manager at the cabaret show at The Castaways Night Club in Birmingham, he joined Derek Salberg's repertory company at the Alexandra Theatre, also in Birmingham, as Assistant Stage Manager, though his ambitions lay as an actor.

After two plays he was appointed Stage Manager and during the season toured regularly to Leeds and appeared in *According to the Evidence* and *No Fear or Favour. According to the Evidence* eventually transferred to the West End of London (John's part being played by the author's son!), although a home-movie featuring John included in the play was never remade and so he achieved a nine-month run at the West End's Savoy Theatre whilst at the same time stage-directing a pantomime with Dick Emery at Wolverhampton's Grand Theatre and acting and stage managing at the Everyman Theatre, Cheltenham. Since then he has always loved doing two things at the same time.

It took John just three years to realise he was not a tremendously gifted performer, so he joined BBC TV in December 1968 as a Floor Assistant, the most junior member of a Production Team. He worked on a tremendously wide variety of shows: *The Benny Hill Show*, *The Tenant of Wildfell Hall*, *The Six Wives of Henry VIII*, *Nationwide*, *Blue Peter*, *The Sky at Night*, *The Morecambe and Wise Show* and three *Doctor Who* series – 'The Space Pirates' with Patrick Troughton, 'Colony in Space' and 'The Ambassadors of Death' with Jon Pertwee.

After two and a half years he became Assistant Floor Manager in Drama Serials working on *Owen M.D.*, *Z Cars* and *The Hole in the Wall*. He was then promoted to Production Assistant on *The Pallisers*, *Barlow At Large*, *The Venturers*, *How Green was my Valley*, and then became a Production Unit Manager (now called Production Associate) on *Flesh and Blood*, two series of *Angels*, three series of *All Creatures Great and Small* and three series of *Doctor Who* with Graham Williams as Producer.

In 1979 JNT (as he is known to almost everyone – among other things!) took over as the producer of *Doctor Who* and is the longest running producer to date. He has the distinction of casting three Doctors – Peter Davison, Colin Baker and Richard Hurndall and apart from the regular seasons of *Doctor Who*, produced 'The Five Doctors' and the spin-off, *K9 and Company*.

John returns to the theatre regularly, both as a member of the audience and as writer/director/producer. In 1973 he wrote and directed *Cinderella* at the Theatre Royal, Drury Lane, which I choreographed.

JNT's Hawaiian shirts are seen regularly at conventions in the UK, the US and Australia and he has appeared on countless radio and TV shows in America, as well as *Saturday Superstore*, *Take Two*, and *Blue Peter* in Britain.

Hawaiian Soup

Serves 6 people

Ingredients:

2 × 15 oz/425 g tins of chilled Vichyssoise soup
1 large tub single (light) cream
1 small tub double cream
1 large tub of soured cream
½ lb/226 g peeled prawns (shelled shrimps)
1 generous tsp bottled mint sauce concentrate
Salt and freshly milled pepper
Chopped chives

Method:

Mix the soup, single cream, double cream and soured cream in a large tureen. Stir to a smooth consistency or blend.

Add the prawns and mint sauce concentrate. Stir to distribute, but do not blend. Place in fridge for 1½ hours. Serve in chilled cups with chopped chives.

Author's Note

This is a very rich and exotic soup.

The *Doctor Who* Fan Club of America

Ron Katz

The *Doctor Who* Fan Club of America was started in 1981 by Ron Katz and Chad Roark. From humble beginnings the Fan Club soon became the biggest *Doctor Who* fan club in the world with over 8,000 members across the United States. Their conventions – or 'Whovian' Festivals – attract people of all ages and from all walks of life. Their energy and enthusiasm for the show is unbounded and they are helping to make *Doctor Who* one of the most popular programmes on American television today.

South Western Gallifrey Corn Soup

Serves 6 people

Ingredients:

7 oz/3½ cups/700 g corn
8 fl oz/½ pint/¼ litre chicken stock (bouillon)
2 oz/56 g butter
16 fl oz/2 cups/½ litre milk
1 crushed clove of garlic
1 tsp/1¼ tsp/7.5 g oregano
Salt and pepper, to taste
1–2 tbs/1¼–2½ tbs 30–60 g canned chillies (rinsed and diced)
1 whole cooked chicken breast (boned and chopped)
1 cup of raw diced tomatoes
4 oz/113 g grated Montaroy Sackminster or Fontina cheese (or cheddar)
2 tbs/2½ tbs/60 g chopped parsley

Method:

Purée the corn and chicken stock in a blender. Combine the butter and the corn purée in a pan and simmer slowly for 5 minutes. Keep stirring, otherwise the corn will stick to the bottom of the pan. Add the milk, garlic, oregano, salt and pepper and bring to the boil.

Reduce the heat and add the chillies and simmer for 5 minutes. This can now be frozen or kept in a refrigerator until needed. When serving, reheat the soup slowly and divide the chicken pieces and tomatoes equally between 6 bowls. Remove the soup from the heat and add the cheese, stirring until the cheese melts. Pour into the bowls and sprinkle with the chopped parsley.

Author's Note:

This is a delicious soup. Every time I go to the USA I try to eat this at least once.

APPETISERS AND SAVOURIES

Verity Lambert

First producer of Doctor Who

Verity Lambert was born in London on November 27. She entered TV in 1954 and her extensive work as a producer in television includes *Doctor Who*, *Adam Adamant Lives*, *Detective*, *Somerset Maughan*, *Shoulder to Shoulder*, (starring Sian Phillips) *Budgie* and *Between the Wars*.

In 1974 she became Controller of Drama for Thames Television and in 1979 Chief Executive for Euston Films. She became Director of Production for Thorn EMI Films Ltd in 1983, relinquishing her position as Controller of Drama for Thames TV but retaining her position as Chief Executive of Euston Films.

Here is Verity Lambert's dish which is one of her favourites.

Hot Potato Salad

Serves 6 people

Ingredients:

2 lb/906 g new potatoes
2 large Spanish onions (roughly chopped)
½ lb/226 g streaky bacon (cut off rind and cut into small strips)
Small jar of mayonnaise
1 oz/28 g butter
1 tsp/1¼ tsp/6.2 ml olive oil
Celery seed
Salt
Freshly ground pepper, to taste

Method:

Part boil the potatoes with their skins until they are soft but not completely cooked. Peel and slice the potatoes approximately one eighth of an inch thick. Cook the bacon in the olive oil and butter until it is fairly crisp then allow to cool.

Into a shallow oven-proof dish which has been greased with the mayonnaise put a layer of potatoes. Sprinkle with celery seed, salt and pepper and some of the onion. Continue until all the potatoes have been used up. Mix cooked bacon and fat with the mayonnaise and pour over the top of the last layer of potatoes.

Place in the oven which has been pre-heated to 375–400°F, 190–200°C (Gas Mark 5–6). Cook for about 30–40 minutes. Take care that it does not dry up: if it looks too dry add a little more mayonnaise, and serve.

Author's Note:

This dish is very good with plain grilled or roasted meat, or as a side dish for a barbeque. It could of course, be eaten as a meal in itself if you feel that way inclined. I think a lovely Rioja would make a good accompaniment to this Hot Potato Salad.

Richard Hurndall

The first Doctor

Richard Hurndall was born on November 3, 1910 in Darlington, County Durham. He studied music in Paris before deciding to be an actor, and then trained at the Royal Academy of Dramatic Art, making his stage debut in 1933, since when he has appeared in many reps (stock) including the Stratford-Upon-Avon Memorial Theatre, and has toured in plays. He also appeared in many West End productions such as *The Affair*, *The New Men*, *The Masters*, *Hostile Witness*, *Justice is a Woman*, and *Highly Confidential*. He was also a former member of the BBC drama rep company, and has appeared frequently on TV in *Z Cars*, *Softly Softly*, *Doctor Finlay's Casebook*, *Callan*, *The Avengers*, *The Power Game*, *It's Murder But Is It Art?*, *The Inheritors*, *The Onedin Line*, *Van Der Valk*, *War and Peace*, *Public Eye*, *Hadleigh*, *The Protectors*, *Enemy at the Door*, and *Philby, Burgess and Maclean*. He recreated the role of William Hartnell's Doctor in 'The Five Doctors'.

Richard's star sign was Scorpio. His hobbies were genealogy, bridge and walking. It was a tragic loss to the acting profession when Richard Hurndall died in 1984 after a long illness. He wrote to me from hospital four days before he died with the recipe that follows. I met him only once at the party to launch 'The Five Doctors'. He was very charming and gentle, and was overwhelmed with the fans' reaction to his portrayal of the first Doctor.

Chicken Mousse

Ingredients:

2 oz/56 g butter
3 oz/85 g white breadcrumbs
1/4 pt/5 oz/1 1/2 dl single (light) cream
8 oz/229 g chopped chicken
3 eggs
3 tbs/3 3/4 tbs/57 ml dry sherry
Salt, to taste
Nutmeg, to taste

Method:

Melt the butter in a basin over a pan of boiling water. To the melted butter add the breadcrumbs, cream and salt, and a good pinch of nutmeg. Stir for 5 minutes. As the mixture thickens, add the 3 eggs and sherry, beat together well and finally put in the chopped chicken. Pour the mixture into a buttered mould or soufflé dish, and cover with tinfoil (aluminium foil), and bake in an oven 350°F 180°C (Gas Mark 4) until firm (about 1/2 hour).

Let it cool and serve chilled with mayonnaise blended together with chopped avocado. You can give your avocado sauce a creamy texture by folding in some stiffly beaten egg white.

Author's Note:

This is not a typical mousse as it is more substantial in texture. However I think it is a perfect starter for any summer or winter evening. I would make this well in advance of use and perhaps serve it with hot garlic bread, or a small mixed salad.

Janet Fielding

Tegan – companion to the fourth and fifth Doctors

Janet Fielding was born in Australia, and went to university to become a journalist, but became involved with student drama and professional theatre. She finished her BA and it was then that she decided to become an actress and joined the travelling theatre called 'Popular Troupe', and toured around Australia. It was in 1977 when the company were touring around England that they played two seasons at the famous Round House theatre in London. Janet decided to stay on in England and joined the Science Fiction Theatre in Liverpool. She has appeared in the opera *The Case of Charles Dexter Ward* in Liverpool and at the ICA in London.

Janet has appeared in the TV series *Shelley*, *Minder*, and *Hammer House of Horror* in England, but she is best known for her role as Tegan in *Doctor Who*, which made her a household name. She joined the programme in 'Logopolis', and remained for nineteen stories, leaving in 'Resurrection of the Daleks'.

Janet is married to Fleet Street journalist, Nick Davies. I went to her wedding and she looked marvellous. She's a great friend of mine and has a super sense of humour.

Janet's recipes reflect her love of good times and I hope you find them fun to prepare.

Fielding's Favourite Soufflé

Ingredients:

1 tb/1¼ tb/30 g butter
2 tbs/2½ tbs/60 g plain flour
¾ pt/15 oz/4½ dl scalded milk
½ tsp/1¼ tsp/3 g salt
¼ tsp/¼ tsp/1 g paprika
Pinch of cayenne
3 rashers (slices) of bacon
4 oz/113 g Gruyère cheese
5 egg yolks
6 egg whites

Method:

Pre-heat the oven to 375°F, 190°C (Gas Mark 5). Place a collar of waxed paper around the outside of a buttered two-pint soufflé dish, and secure it with a piece of string. Lightly grill the three rashers of bacon and grate the cheese, then separate the eggs. Melt the butter over a low heat, stir in the flour and cook, stirring constantly for one minute.

Gradually add the scalded milk and then remove from the heat. Add the cheese and bacon to the mixture and stir well until the cheese has melted.

Beat in the egg yolks in a small bowl and add three tablespoons of the mixture to the egg yolks and blend well. Return the egg yolks to the mixture in the saucepan and blend thoroughly. Then add the salt, cayenne and paprika and set the mixture aside to cool. Meanwhile take a medium-sized non-stick plastic bowl and wipe the inside with a kitchen towel dampened with vinegar. Put the egg whites in the bowl and beat until stiff. Take a metal spoon and gently fold the egg whites into the cheese and bacon mixture. Pour into the soufflé dish and bake in the oven for 35–40 minutes.

Author's note:

Soufflés are difficult to make. However this one is really worth the effort. It is too delicious to ignore. I suggest a Cheverny 1982/3 VDQS wine to accompany this dish – this is a crisp, dry wine.

Johnny Byrne

Writer for Doctor Who

Johnny Byrne is one of England's top writers today, having many films, TV shows and novels to his credit. Some of his films include *Adolf Hitler – My Part in his Downfall*, *Perdita* and *Xtro II* (the sequel to *Xtro*). His TV shows include *Space 1999*, *Season of the Witch*, *Day After Tomorrow*, *All Creatures Great and Small*, *Doctor Who*, *Tales of the Unexpected*, *World of Rhythm*, *Miracles Take Longer* and *One by One*. His books include *Best of Science Fiction*, and *Groupie*. I worked with Johnny on *All Creatures Great and Small*, when I was an Assistant Floor Manager, and we have been friends ever since.

Whenever Johnny visits the BBC TV centre I end up in the pub across the road for a lunchtime constitutional!

Kipper of Traken

Serves 4 people

Ingredients:

8 kipper fillets (approximately ¾ lb/350 g)
6 fl oz/6½ oz/175 ml mild olive oil
2 fl oz/¼ cup/55 ml wine vinegar
1 dessertspoon brown sugar
2 bay leaves
1 heaped tsp/1¼ tsp/30 g mustard powder
1 medium sized onion, sliced
2 tsps/2½ tsps/60 g crushed coriander seeds
Freshly milled black pepper
Lemon slices and watercress for garnish

Method:
Turn the kipper fillets upside down on a flat surface, and, using a sharp knife to help you, take off the skins. In a 1½ pint oval dish, layer the fillets with slices of onion and a sprinkling of coriander and black pepper, tucking in the two bayleaves. In a screw top jar, dissolve mustard powder and sugar in the vinegar and olive oil. Screw on the lid and shake vigorously, then pour the mixture over the fillets. Cover carefully with a lid or cling-film. Leave to marinate in the lowest part of the fridge for 4 days. Garnish and serve with thinly sliced bread and butter.

Author's Note:
Most favoured dish of the Keepers of Traken. The nearest earthbound equivalent to the smoked Katura Kipper, so popular that many Trakens took their given names from it, is the delicious Arbroath Smokie. The recipe was found among the possessions abandoned by Nyssa on the TARDIS.

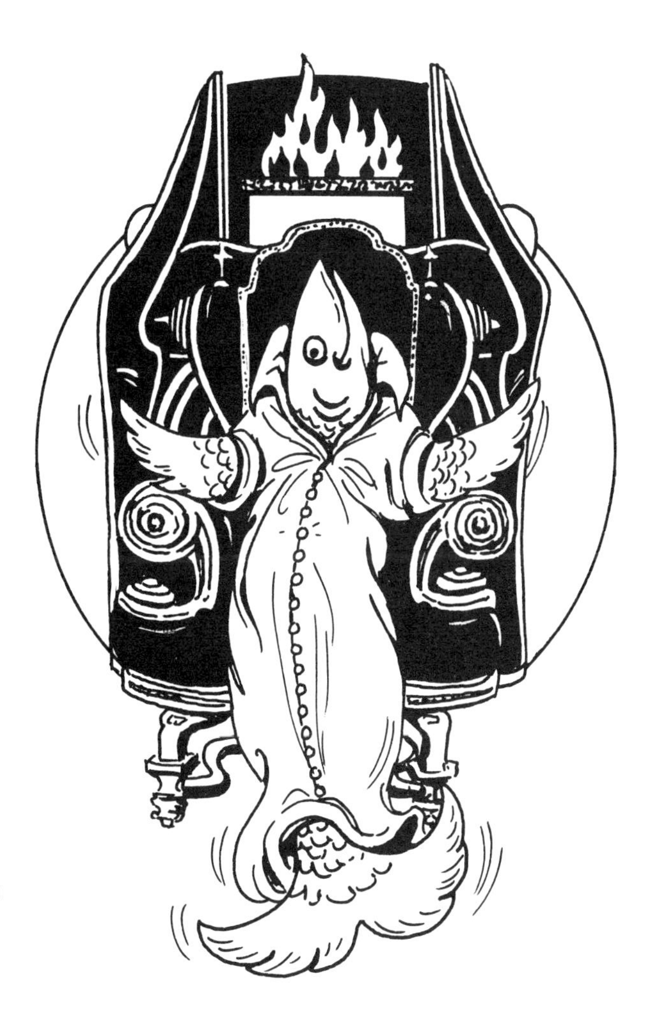

Valentine Dyall

Black Guardian

Valentine Dyall is the son of the late actor, Franklyn Dyall. Valentine was born in London and educated at Harrow and Christchurch, Oxford. He became famous through the long running series on radio called *Appointment with Fear* and through this became known as 'The Man in Black'.

Valentine has always been associated with serious plays and the classics. His acting career started at the Old Vic Theatre and his first major film was Laurence Olivier's *Henry V* in which he played the Duke of Burgundy.

His fans will be surprised to learn that Valentine had a long association with Spike Milligan and the Goons in *Idiots Weekly* and he has appeared with the arch Goon Milligan in *Son of Oblomov* and *The Bedsitting Room*. His TV appearances have been numerous and include *Secret Army*, *O.9*, *Blake's Seven*, *The Hitchhikers Guide To The Galaxy*, *Nanny*, and, of course, *Doctor Who* as the famous Black Guardian. His most recent appearances have included the title role in the thriller *The Lodger*, and every Christmas he dons the role of Abanazer in the pantomime *Aladdin*.

When I met Valentine I found him to be highly intelligent, charming and very friendly, despite that daunting rich-brown voice. He has a son, Christian, who is a costume designer for BBC TV.

Moules à la Gardienne Noire

Ingredients:

25 shelled mussels
3½ oz/100 g butter
1–1½ cloves of garlic
1 handful fresh parsley
Salt and pepper
Nutmeg (optional)
Mashed potatoes (either instant or freshly mashed, and enough for 6 people)

Method:

To make the garlic butter, peel the cloves of garlic and crush, or pound with a mortar. Blend together the butter and crushed garlic, so that the garlic completely impregnates the butter. Cut the parsley as finely as you can, and add to the butter so that it is distributed evenly throughout. Add a little salt and pepper and nutmeg (the nutmeg can be omitted, according to taste).

Make sure that the mashed potatoes have been prepared beforehand and put them into small flat dishes to a thickness of about 1½ in. Scoop out the mashed potatoes and put a mussel in each. Top up the holes with garlic butter and place in a very hot oven 450–470°F, 230–240°C, (Gas Mark 8–9) for about 10 to 15 minutes, until the garlic butter has completely melted. Then sprinkle chopped parsley over the whole dish as a garnish.

Author's Note:

A lovely shellfish dish to be eaten when in season. The black shells of the mussels give an air of mystery. Can also be eaten as a main meal as well.

As Valentine Dyall said 'It is basically a question of treating mussels as if they were snails.' I have had this dish and it is indeed delicious. Make sure that the mussels are really fresh and you will enjoy a lovely dish.

Mary Tamm

Romana – first incarnation

Mary Tamm joined *Doctor Who* in the sixteenth season, her first story being 'The Ribos Operation'. She then subsequently appeared in 'The Pirate Planet', 'The Stones of Blood', 'The Androids of Tara', 'The Power of Kroll' and 'The Armageddon Factor'.

Mary has appeared in many stage productions throughout the British Isles, including the West End of London. She starred in the film, *The Odessa File*, and her TV credits include *The Assassination Run*, *Jane Eyre* and *The Hello, Goodbye Man*.

She has also been busy with her young daughter and her new house. Her husband, Marcus, works in the City of London, dealing in high finance.

Mary, Marcus and I had a fabulous time in Chicago during the twentieth anniversary celebrations in November 1984. We particularly enjoyed the shopping. We kept bumping into each other in various stores, and it looked as if Mary was trying to buy out the stores.

Mary has suggested a very refreshing appetiser.

Time Lady Tzaziki

Serves 4 people

Ingredients:

½ medium cucumber, skinned and roughly diced
Salt and freshly ground black pepper
5 oz/143 g natural yoghurt
1 garlic clove, skinned and crushed
1 tb/1¼ tb/30 g chopped fresh mint

Method:
Place the cucumber in a colander, sprinkle with salt and leave to stand for 30 minutes to draw out the juices. Rinse, drain well and dry with absorbent kitchen paper. Place in a serving bowl. Pour over the yoghurt, add the garlic, mint, seasoning and mix well. Cover and chill in the refrigerator for 30–60 minutes to allow the flavours to develop.

Serve with hot pitta bread.

Author's Note:
This dish is pronounced *zat-zee-kee* and is a perfect starter to a summer meal. The yoghurt and mint add a delicate taste. One of my favourites.

Philip Latham

Borusa in 'The Five Doctors'

Philip Latham was born at Leigh-on-Sea, Essex on January 17. He was educated at Feltstead School. After National Service he trained as an actor at RADA and then went into the theatre at Farnham.

His most recent stage work includes *The Winslow Boys* and *The Letter*, which were both National Tours. He has also appeared in the films, *Spy Story*, *Force Ten from Navarone*, and *Man from a Far Country*.

Philip Latham is also very well known for his appearance on British TV in *Mogul*, *The Trouble Shooters*, *Maigret*, *Whose Life is it Anyway?*, *No Exit*, *Time Lock*, *Good at Games*, *The Pallisers*, *The Cedar Tree*, *The Professionals*, *The Killers*, *Hammer House of Horror*, *Name for the Day*, *Nanny*, *Number 10* as Wellington, *The Fourth Arm*, and, of course, in his role as Lord President Borusa in *Doctor Who*.

Philip is also in great demand for his religious reading. His star sign is Capricorn and his hobbies are playing cricket, and the Royal Academy of Dramatic Art in London.

Philip's recipe involves peppers!

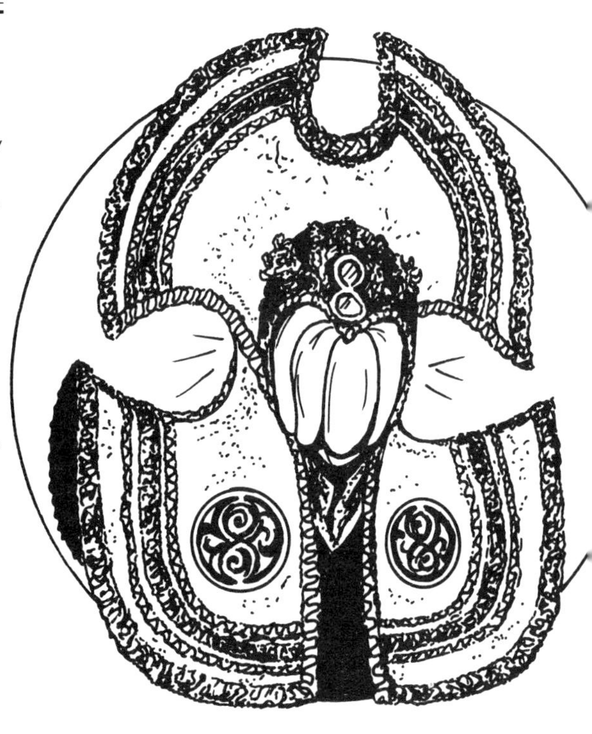

Borusa Peppers

Ingredients:

4 green peppers
8 oz/229 g rice
1 crushed clove of garlic
Chopped olives
Chopped anchovy fillets
Salt and pepper
½ pt/10 oz/3 dl tomato soup

Method:

Get a Cyberman to remove the top of each pepper and scoop out the seeds (making sure that the pepper is intact), then put the peppers in a pan of water and bring to the boil. Remove the peppers when the water is boiling. Drain the peppers carefully through a Dalek head, or a colander, whichever happens to be more readily available, and then stand each pepper upright in an oven-proof dish.

Mix together the cooked rice, crushed garlic, chopped olives and chopped anchovies (*any Time Lord can chop anything!*). Season well or to taste, and fill each pepper with the mixture. Surround each pepper with ½ in of tomato soup. Cover the whole dish with tinfoil (aluminium foil) and cook in the oven at 375°F, 190°C (Gas Mark 5) for 15 minutes. Guaranteed instant petrifaction of eternity.

Author's Note:

On earth this is known as Stuffed Peppers. I love them but I must say that until I tried this dish, I had never tried peppers stuffed with anchovies. However I found the somewhat Moorish taste delicious.

Stratford Johns

Monarch in 'Four to Doomsday'

Stratford Johns was born in South Africa and started working in films and TV in 1948. He became famous in the well-known British TV series *Z Cars* and *Softly Softly*, in which he played Inspector Barlow, a role he later revived in the hugely successful *Barlow at Large*. These series were sold abroad and in Australia Stratford became a star. I first met Alan, as he's known to friends, backstage in his dressing-room at the Duke of Yorks theatre in the West End of London during a small party after the show on the eve of Stratford's departure to do a season in Australia with the play. It was an enormous success. Stratford Johns once again gave a very good performance as Monarch in 'Four to Doomsday' and his make-up and costume were brilliant.

There was one funny moment when Alan came into the BBC Club in his outdoor clothes with his frog face make-up on. I can honestly say that a few people stopped drinking immediately, as they were under the impression that they were having the DTs! It *did* look very funny. Stratford Johns has decided to keep the Monarch theme for his starter recipe for Frogs' Legs, which I find delicious.

Here for your taste-buds is Frogs' Legs à la Provençale'. *Bon Appetit*!

Frogs' Legs à la Provençale

Ingredients:

2 lb/906 g medium sized frogs' legs
8 oz/229 g butter
1 tb/1¼ tb/19 ml olive oil
1 tb/1¼ tb/30 g finely chopped parsley
2 cloves of finely chopped garlic
¼ pt/5 oz/1½ dl milk
2 tbs/2½ tbs/30 g chopped chives
Salt and pepper
Juice of ½ lemon
Small amount of flour

Method:

Add the salt and the pepper to the milk and dip the frogs' legs into the milk. Then roll them in the flour. Heat 2 oz of butter in a large frying pan with the olive oil, add the frogs' legs and gently fry for 12 minutes until the frogs' legs are browned. Add the lemon juice, parsley, chives, and a pinch of pepper. Stir this with the frogs' legs and keep them warm in a serving dish.

Add the remaining butter and the garlic, and brown quickly. Then pour over the frogs' legs in the serving dish. Cut slices of lemon and use as a garnish.

Janet Fielding

Fielding's Ocker Balls

Ingredients:

Pastry
½ pt/10 oz/3 dl water
3 oz/85 g butter, cut into pieces
1 tsp/1¼ tsp/7.5 g salt
Pinch of pepper
Pinch of nutmeg
4 oz/113 g sifted flour
4 × 2 oz/56 g eggs

Method:
Bring the water slowly to the boil with the butter and seasonings until the butter has melted. Remove from the heat and pour in all the flour quickly. Beat vigourously with a wooden spoon until blended thoroughly. Then beat over a moderately high heat for a couple of minutes until the mixture leaves the side of the pan. Remove the saucepan from the heat and make a well in the centre of the mixture. Break an egg into the well and beat it until it is absorbed into the mixture. Continue with the rest of the eggs beating them in one by one. Place little balls of pastry on a well-buttered baking sheet. Space them well apart. Place in a pre-heated oven at 425°F, 220°C, (Gas Mark 7) for about 20 minutes.

Filling
Ingredients:

½ lb//229 g Philadelphia cream cheese
1 small can smoked oysters
4 oz/113 g prawns (shrimps)
Lemon juice
Single (light) cream
Black lumpfish roe

Method:
Mix the cream cheese with a little of the cream. Add the oysters and prawns and some lemon juice. Season and fill the pastry balls with it. Garnish the top with black lumpfish roe.

Author's Note:
A very exotic dish, as can be expected from Janet, for when you are feeling rich. As for wine I suggest a chilled bottle of champagne, such as 'Alfred Gratien Cremant Brut 1976' which is a very good vintage and quite reasonably priced.

Mark Strickson

Turlough – companion to the fifth Doctor

I first met Mark when we were both working on a TV series called *Angels* in which Mark played the part of an ambulance driver. (The series dealt with the everyday running of a hospital and the lives of its nurses.) We got on well together instantly, having a lot of laughs in between takes on the set.

A few months later I happened to see Mark in the BBC TV Reception at Shepherds Bush, waiting to be interviewed for the role of the new male companion in *Doctor Who*. There were hundreds of young actors hoping to get this most sought-after role, and I was very pleased to hear that Mark had landed the part. He is a very good actor. As Turlough you loved to hate him, and never quite trusted him. He was not what he seemed. Mark's interpretation of the part was inspired and with those weird eyebrows the make-up department designed he brought a new dimension to the style of companions of *Doctor Who*.

Mark and his lovely wife Julie Brennon (who is an actress) have a delightful apartment on the south side of the River Thames, very near the famous Old Vic Theatre. However Mark and Julie spend most of their time on their boat on the River Thames near the Chelsea Embankment. Mark is also an accomplished musician playing a number of instruments and singing as well. Mark and Julie have a great *joie de vivre* – they even cycle in the centre of London! Later this year (1985) Mark will be seen as the young Scrooge in a new movie version of the Charles Dickens classic *A Christmas Carol*.

Here is Mark's salad 'for those languid summer days or nights'.

One O'Clock Salad

Serves 2 people

('A quiet snack for the lunchtime when you have missed the morning and wish that the afternoon was not there either')

Ingredients:

1 Chinese lettuce (or any crisp lettuce)
Fresh hard tomatoes
4 oz/113 g bacon strips (remove the rind)
3 eggs
Salt and pepper
1 oz/28 g unsalted butter
3 oz (85 g) walnut halves
Vinaigrette (2 parts oil and 1 part lemon juice, salt and pepper)

Method:

First put the oven on low. Heat the grill for the bacon.

1) Prepare the lettuce and the tomatoes in a bowl cutting the lettuce into mouth-sized pieces. This could be done to the tomatoes as well. (Do this as quietly and humanely as possible.)

2) Grill the bacon strips until they are well crisped (but not burned), and put them into the oven to keep warm.

3) Beat the eggs (gently), and add the salt and pepper and also a tablespoon of water.

4) Melt the butter in an omelette pan, add the egg and cook by easing the omelette away from the edge of the pan allowing the uncooked egg to run into the resulting crevasse.

5) When well cooked slide out of the pan onto a large plate and cut into strips.

6) Dress the salad with the vinaigrette dressing at the last moment, and scatter the nuts on the top of it, then the bacon pieces, and finally arrange the omelette strips on individual plates if so desired, or on one large plate.

Suggested wine: any crisp dry white wine served very chilled, for example, Sauvignon or a Muscadet, or for the very weak, a bottle of sparkling spring water.

Author's Note:

This dish is definitely for the 18 year olds and over. I also suggest that if you arrive at a venue and the following meal preparations are in progress, well, you only live once!

Ingrid Pitt

Doctor Solow in 'Warriors of the Deep'

Ingrid Pitt is an actress and writer. She made her acting debut with the Berlin Ensemble, and appeared in many of their productions such as *The Caucasian Chalk Circle* and *Night Asylum*. She has made many films, her international debut being in 1968 with *Where Eagles Dare*. Her other films include *The Vampire Lovers*, *The House that Dripped Blood* (with Jon Pertwee) and *Countess Dracula*.

I first met Ingrid Pitt in the late 1960s when I was a dancer. I was called in by a choreographer to partner Ingrid for a screen test for a major film. The original dancer had injured himself in the middle of the test, and had been despatched to hospital. After a frantic twenty minute rehearsal, the cameras rolled. The music started and Ingrid and I waltzed around the movie set, and as the last strains of the waltz died down I swept Ingrid into my arms and experienced my very first screen kiss with one of the world's leading screen sex symbols. I shall always remember that kiss.

Doctor Solow's Specials

Ingrid Pitt's idea of a perfect meal is an *Asado*, or barbeque, gleaned from the Gauchos in South America. They barbeque everything, from meatballs to whole turkeys. Ingrid has derived a special *Katuschi* for barbequeing. However on special Solow nights with Solow guests she might serve the following menu:

As *Zakuschi* (hors d'oeuvre), Blinis with caviar and sour cream. (If not inundated with filmparts Ingrid Pitt will substitute caviar with lumpfish.) or she might choose Razumovski Salad as the entrée.

For the main meal she favours Zraza with red cabbage and boiled potatoes. The trick to Zraza (beef meat rolls) is the rich gravy in combination with the red cabbage soaked into the boiled potatoes.

For cheese, Ingrid Pitt would choose goat cheese and black bread or pumpernickel, but never biscuits. *Everybody* serves biscuits and saltless butter.

Here then is the first course for you to make:

Blinis

The following quantities make about 32 Blinis

Ingredients:

1 lb 9 oz/700 g plain sifted flour
1¾ oz/50 g fresh yeast or 4 packets of dried yeast
1¼ pt/25 oz/7 dl warm water
1¾ oz/50 g melted butter
3 eggs
1 tb/1¼ tb/30 g salt
1 oz/25 g sugar
1 pt/20 oz/6 dl milk
Butter or oil for frying
Red or black caviar
Sour cream

Method:

Mix the yeast with a little warm water until it becomes a smooth paste. Add the rest of the warm water, and half of the sifted flour, and mix with a wooden spoon. Cover the mixing bowl and leave it in a warm place for about half an hour so that the yeast can rise. It should rise to approximately double its volume and be full of bubbles. (Make sure that your mixing bowl is large enough.)

Gradually add the rest of the flour, beating until the mixture is smooth. Stir in the melted butter, then add the egg yolks (having first separated the yolk from the egg white) and the sugar and salt. Warm the milk and gradually add this to the batter until the batter becomes smooth. Leave once again in a warm place to rise for a second time.

Beat the egg whites until they stand in peaks and fold them in after the mixture has once again doubled. Allow this to rise for a third time. The batter should be full of bubbles. Heat two small thick-based frying pans and brush them with the melted butter or oil. Pour a tablespoon of batter into the frying pans.

The Blini should be very thin when cooked and full of holes like lace. The first Blinis are often rather too thick and can be discarded. If the batter seems too thick, a little more warm milk can be added carefully. Keep the first Blini in a warm oven while you are frying the others. The rest of the batter can be left for a short time while you are eating the first batch. Eat with Red or Black Caviar and sour cream.

Author's Note:
I found that the ideal size of a Blini is the size of a very small plate. Then when the caviar and sour cream are added it is more manageable to eat. I roll it up, and drink Vodka, Russian style (neat), or champagne with this dish. I usually find that I can cope with about four, and it is very good as a snack or light meal on a lovely afternoon or a summer evening with a group of friends. To be eaten when you have a special occasion.

Razumovski Salad

Ingredients:

2 hardboiled eggs
2 large or 4 small boiled beetroots
4 medium sized boiled potatoes
4 sour dill pickles
6 fillets of pickled herring
4 large cooking apples
3 medium onions
Sour cream or mayonnaise
Vinegar
Salt

Method:
Peel and boil the potatoes and then cut them into oblong pieces. Slice the pickles and cut into strips. Peel and dice the cooked beetroot. Drain the herrings from their liquid, and cut into squares. (Keep the herring juice or marinade for the dressing.) Peel and chop the boiled eggs. Remove the peel from the apples and the onions, and then chop and dice them. Mix all the ingredients together in a large mixing bowl. Add the sour cream and mix with the marinade or herring juice until they have combined thoroughly. (One can use mayonnaise instead of sour cream.) Add the vinegar if the dressing is not savoury enough. Pour over the salad and toss thoroughly.

Author's Note:
This could also be eaten as a main meal for lunch. It may be a bit too savoury for people with a sweet tooth, but it is extremely tasty. I would recommend a lovely dry white wine (or sparkling rosé) with this salad.

Matthew Robinson

Director of 'Resurrection of the Daleks' and 'Attack of the Cybermen'

Matthew has been directing popular TV drama since 1973. His credits include *Z Cars*, *Softly, Softly*, *Angels* and *Doctor Who*, for BBC TV, *Coronation Street*, *Emmerdale Farm*, and *Crown Court* for ITV, and *Brookside* for Channel 4. Before he directed drama, Matthew worked on BBC TV Current Affairs programmes including *Nationwide* and *The Money Programme*.

Matthew lives in a fashionable cul-de-sac in Fulham, London and drives a BMW motor car. He likes playing the piano (he is a very good musician), films, backgammon, chess, word processors, tennis, jogging (he ran in the London Marathon in May 1984), advanced cooking, writing plays and cats. He does not like tomatoes and dogs.

Doctor Who's Soft Planet Landing

Serves 4 people

Ingredients:

2 semi-soft avocados
1 medium melon (honeydew or ogen)
1 cucumber
2 tbs/2½ tbs/60 g small walnut pieces
Dressing (French or English, according to taste)

Method:
Slice the avocados in half and remove the stones. Carefully remove the flesh from the skins and cut the halves into teaspoon-sized pieces. Place them in a serving dish.

Quarter the melon, remove the seeds and the skin, and then cut it into pieces slightly larger than the avocados. Place these in the serving dish as well.

Remove an inch or so from either end of the cucumber, and pare off the skin leaving only a thin strip of skin running down the length of the cucumber. Slice into chunky cubes, similar in size to the melon pieces. Place them in the serving bowl as well.

Scatter walnut pieces into the dish and cover. Shake the dish gently to thoroughly mix the ingredients together. Leave covered until just before you want to serve. Remove the cover and sprinkle the dressing over the fruit, nut and cucumber mixture. Serve at once. *Do not put the dish into the fridge.*

Author's Note:
An easy to prepare starter using melon, avocado and cucumber, this is one of those dishes that gives two different tastes. The sweetness of the fruits combines wonderfully well with the tartness of the dressing.

Adrienne Corri

Mena in 'The Leisure Hive'

Adrienne Corri is one of our best known actresses. She has appeared in countless movies, TV, and theatre productions and has appeared in the West End of London in leading roles on many occasions.

When Adrienne appeared in 'The Leisure Hive', a query was brought up as to the logistics of tachyonics which was the theme of the story. It was then discovered that Adrienne is an avid reader of all the major science fiction magazines and books, as well as taking an active interest in extra-terrestrial sightings. She is also very well read on US Space projects, and tachyonics is one of her pet subjects. In sixty seconds she had solved the problem and no one dared query her answer (which was perfectly correct).

Recently Adrienne has found herself in another role as an advisor to Sotheby's and Christie's, the two major art houses in the world. She is an expert on the artist, Gainsborough, and recently discovered and had authenticated a painting that had hung for years above the bar in a theatre in Birmingham. She has devoted years of research to this subject and is now considered an expert.

Adrienne has yet another talent – as a playwright. She has written a 'Whodunnit' for the theatre which

has had an extensive national tour, and at the time of writing is to open in London's West End.

As Adrienne is of Italian extraction she has given a rather delicious Bolognese sauce for you to try.

Mena's Tachyonic Sauce

Serves 6–8 people

Ingredients:

2 lb/906 g tomatoes
2 tbs/2½ tbs/38 ml oil (vegetable or olive)
2 large mild onions
2 cloves of garlic (chopped or crushed)
1 bay leaf
1 tsp/1¼ tsp/7.5 g curry powder
Pinch of sugar
1 large green pepper
A few coriander seeds
1 salt spoon of grated nutmeg
1 cup of white stock
1 large glass of red wine
1 lb/453 g minced (chopped) beef
Salt and pepper to taste
2 tbs/2½ tbs/38 ml tomato purée (paste)
Juice of 1 lemon

Method:

First fry the chopped garlic with the curry powder. Peel the tomatoes and set aside. Chop into pieces.

Fry the onions and the green peppers, both of which should have been sliced finely, until soft. Put the chopped beef into the pan and brown it with the vegetables, and add the herbs. Stir until all the meat is brown.

Add the pieces of tomato, the wine and the stock. Simmer gently for half an hour, keeping the lid on the pan. Make sure the sauce does not stick to the bottom of the pan, or does not get too thick. Stir and add more red wine if this seems to be happening. Don't mash up the tomatoes. Add the tomato purée and the lemon juice just a few minutes before serving.

Author's Note:

An ideal sauce to accompany Barry Letts' unnamed recipe, to be found in the Vegetarian Dishes section. The longer you let this cook the better it tastes. I tend to make my pasta sauces the day before eating, having cooked them for at least two hours. Then the next day I reheat on a very low heat, stirring continually, and serve.

As this is Italian, let's have an Italian wine to go with this. How about Maso Lodron 1981 (a very fruity wine which will keep well) or Cabernet Riserva del Trentino 1980?

Fiona Cumming

Director of 'Castrovalva', 'Snakedance', 'Enlightenment', 'Planet of Fire'

Fiona was born in Edinburgh, Scotland. She was educated in Edinburgh and Glasgow at the George Warson's Ladies College, and the Glasgow High School for girls. She received her training at Glasgow University, and the Royal Scottish Academy of Music and Drama.

She started her career acting in the theatre and on TV and for a time was a TV announcer and interviewer. Fiona joined the BBC as an assistant floor manager and after a short period became a production manager and then graduated to the position of director.

She left the BBC to become a freelance director. She has recently been hopping between Scottish TV, BBC TV, and Yorkshire TV.

Fiona is married to Ian Fraser, a freelance production manager.

Snakedance Starter

Serves 2 people

Ingredients:

1 ripe avocado
1 iceberg or crisp heart lettuce (any lettuce will do)
2 dessertspoons of caviar (or Danish lumpfish roe)
1 large carton of soured cream

Method:
Take a ripe avocado and halve it, removing the stone and the skin. Place a leaf of lettuce on two plates and place a dessertspoon of caviar or Danish lumpfish roe in the centre of each lettuce leaf. Invert each half avocado over the mound of caviar so that the caviar has filled the space occupied originally by the stone, or pip. Smother the green surface of the avocado with sour cream. Eat with a knife and fork.

Author's Note:
This is an easy to prepare starter which is very tasty.

David Banks

Cyberleader in 'Earthshock', 'The Five Doctors', 'Attack of the Cybermen'

I first met David Banks in the middle of a stone quarry in the freezing cold and mist somewhere in North Wales. The film unit was cold and wet, when I noticed in the freezing fog a group of people with silver helmets and suits who seemed to be quite warm by comparison. Yes, they were the Cybermen. The suits were an ideal barrier against the horrid conditions.

David is a very charming young man and I'm sure that whenever the Cyberleader is required, David will play the part if he is available. He has made it very much his own. Here in David's own words are how the Cyber Race sustain themselves:

'This is a recipe from the Ancient Era of the Great Cyber Race, when some sustenance in the way of orally administered non-mineral matter was required. Of course, even at that early stage the consumption of meat had long been abolished as irrational. It is high in iron content as well as other minerals and salts. Note the large quantity of oil to guard against corrosion.'

Cyberleader Special for Iron Replenishment (High in Iron Content)

Ingredients:

1 medium cauliflower
1 lb/453 g green broccoli
¼pt/5 oz/1½ dl olive oil (or other polyunsaturates)
1 large onion (chopped into chunks)
18 stoned black olives (cut into slices)
1 tin of anchovies (chopped into slices)
4 oz/113 g strong Cheshire cheese or similar
½ pt/1 cup/¼ litre red cooking wine

Method:
Remove the cauliflower and broccoli florets and break into even pieces. Thinly slice the leaves and stalks of the broccoli. Pour 2 oz of oil (2 tablespoons approx US) into a large heavy pan (or pot). A pressure cooker is ideal; although ex-stock Cyber heads were used in the old days. Put the ingredients into the pan in the following order:

1) Half of the onion, with the olives and anchovies (having mixed them together previously).
2) Sliced broccoli leaves and stalks.
3) Half of the grated cheese, and a sprinkling of oil.
4) Put in the remaining half of the onion, olive and anchovy mixture.
5) Put in the broccoli and cauliflower florets and add the remainder of the cheese and oil.
6) Finally pour in the red wine. (Yeast extract in water could be substituted for red wine but this is a nasty corrosive substance for Cybermen.)

Bring to the boil and then simmer with the lid on the pan for about 10 minutes, or until the broccoli and cauliflower florets, are tender. Serve immediately with little cubes of hot buttered toast.

Author's Note:
This could be a first course, but I have found that as a light meal on its own it is quite adequate. It could even be used as a vegetable dish to accompany a main course.

Frazer Hines

Jamie McCrimmon – Companion to the second Doctor

Frazer Hines was born in Harrogate in England. He entered the acting profession in 1952. Frazer joined *Doctor Who* in 'The Highlanders', and was last seen in 'The Two Doctors'. After his initial two and a half years stint in *Doctor Who* Frazer joined the regular cast of Yorkshire TV's *Emmerdale Farm* and stayed with the show for twelve years.

As there is an abundance of mushrooms in Scotland, and Jamie would obviously have had them in his staple diet, here is Frazer's suggestion for a starter. However Frazer told me recently that he is a rotten cook but enjoys cooking this dish because of its simplicity. Apparently he is slowly getting interested in cooking and recommends this dish for beginners.

Mushrooms McCrimmon

Ingredients:

Fresh raw mushrooms (as many as you and the Doctor can eat between you)
Oil or butter
1 tin of anchovies
1 carton of single cream, to taste

Method:
Heat the oil or butter in a large frying pan, and put as many mushrooms as you like (depending on how many people you are entertaining) into the pan and gently fry until they become soft but do not over-cook. Meanwhile, put the anchovies into a blender and blend to a creamy texture. Add the fresh dairy cream and keep adding to taste until the anchovies do not dominate the flavour. Place the mushrooms in a serving dish and pour the mixture over the mushrooms and serve immediately. This dish takes only a few minutes to make.

Author's Note:
This is a very tasty and simple dish to make. It is quick and very economical. If the reader feels in an extravagant mood, slice an avocado pear in half, and fill the halves with Mushrooms McCrimmon.

Martin Jarvis

The Governor in 'Vengeance on Varos'; Butler in 'Invasion of the Dinosaurs'; and Hilio in 'The Web Planet'

Martin Jarvis was born on August 4 in Cheltenham and on leaving school he went to RADA to train as an actor. After completing his training he started at Manchester Rep. While at drama school he won the silver medal and the Vanburgh Award. He returned to London from Manchester and started working in the theatre in *Cockade*, *Poor Bitos*, *Man and Superman*, *The Spoils of Poynton*, *The Bandwagon*, *The Prodigal Daughter*, *The Rivals* (he also appeared in America in this production), and *Hamlet*. He also played Edward VIII in *The Woman I Love* at Bromley, as well as appearing in Canada and Hong Kong in the Arts Festival. His films include *The Last Escape*, *Ike* (in which he played George V), *The Circle*, and *Caught in the Act*. Martin has also performed in numerous radio plays including *War and Peace* and *Great Expectations*.

He does a number of readings and he is also the author of a number of radio plays. His many TV appearances include *The Forsyte Saga*, *Nicholas Nickleby*, *The Pallisers*, *Ross*, *After Liverpool*, *The Samaritan*, *Zigger Zagger*, *True Patriot*, *David Copperfield*, *Killers*, *Charades*, *Enemy at the Door*, *Rings on their Fingers*, *Breakaway*, *The Business of Murder*, *Jackanory*, *The Bunker*, and *Doctor Who*.

The first time that I met Martin I was choreographing *Nicholas Nickleby* for BBC TV, and since then we find that we are always bumping into each other at the BBC Rehearsal Rooms. Martin's star sign is Leo and he was educated at the Whitgift School in Croydon, and then went to London University. He is married to actress Rosalind Ayres and they have two sons. His hobbies are music, Indian food, movies, working, and interior design.

Martin has given a recipe for a meal he had when he was working in Paris. His two sons adore it and he thought that the younger readers might like it.

Croque de Governor or Croque Provençale

Ingredients:

1 medium sliced loaf of bread
Tomatoes
Bacon
Cheddar cheese or red Leicester, or similar
Milk
Rosemary
Tarragon
Black pepper

Method:
Place the slices of cheese in a bowl and cover the cheese with milk. Allow to stand until the cheese has absorbed the milk a little. Having toasted one side of the slices of bread, scoop the slices of cheese out of the milk with the ladle and place on the untoasted side of the bread. The excess milk will be absorbed by the bread. Then place slices of tomato on top of the cheese. (You could do a layer of cheddar then a layer of red Leicester on top to get a mixture of colours.) Then sprinkle the slices with rosemary and tarragon and lots of black pepper. Grill until the cheese is bubbly. A slice of bacon could also be placed on top of the cheese as well. Remember to place the herbs onto the cheese *before* grilling.

Author's Note:
This is an ideal light meal or family snack. It gives the traditional cheese on toast a new dimension.

Lalla Ward

Romana – second incarnation

Lalla Ward was trained at the Central School of Speech and Drama and has appeared in numerous films including *Matushka*, *Vampire Circus*, *England Made Me*, *Got it Made*, *Rosebud* and *The Prince and the Pauper*. Her recent TV work includes *The Ash Tree* in the Ghost Story series, *Quiller*, *Almost Tomorrow* in the Jubilee series, *Hazell*, *Who Pays the Ferryman*, *The Professionals* and BBC TV's *Hamlet*, in which she played Ophelia.

She originally appeared in *Doctor Who* as Princess Astra in 'The Armageddon Factor' and then returned to play Romana Mark 2.

At Lalla's Birthday Party in 1984 I happened to eat the most delicious terrine I had ever tasted. I have persuaded Lalla to let me include it in my book. It is a special dish devised by her father and herself and I strongly recommend it.

E.T.T. (Extra Terrestrial Terrine)

Serves 10–12 people

Ingredients:

1 rabbit (tame or wild) – 1½–2 lb/681–906 g
Same weight of unsalted, streaky pork belly
½ lb/228 g chicken livers
Large handful of parsley
Half a handful of fresh coriander
Handful of shelled pistachio nuts
1 wine glass brandy or, even better, Armagnac
1–1½ lb/453–681 g streaky bacon, without the rind, deboned and sliced thinly for lining the terrine dish
3 large onions
3 cloves of garlic
3 bay leaves
1 dessertspoon each of thyme and basil (fresh if at all possible)
Freshly milled pepper
1 calf's foot to make jelly
1 packet of aspic powder

Method:

Bone the rabbit and chop into large cubes. Put into a mixing bowl and add the pork belly and the chicken livers, all of which must be hand-chopped to the same size.

Finely chop the onions, garlic, parsley and coriander (this can be done in a machine) and add to the bowl. Add the nuts, herbs, brandy and a generous amount of freshly milled pepper. You won't need any salt as there's enough in the bacon. Thoroughly mix the whole lot and leave to marinate.

Meanwhile, heat the oven to 350°F, 180°C (Gas Mark 4). Place the calf's foot in a large saucepan, cover with water, bring to the boil and reduce to make the jelly. Remove from the heat, strain and then add the packet of aspic powder to fortify.

Line the terrine dish with the bacon, leaving enough for the top. Fill the dish with the terrine mixture and press down. Put the bay leaves on top and cover with a herring-bone pattern of bacon.

Pour the liquid aspic all around, put the lid on and place on a baking dish in the middle of the oven. Cook for 1 hour at a moderate temperature and then reduce the oven to 250°F, 120°C (Gas Mark 1–2) and cook for a further hour.

Leave the terrine in the oven after the heat has been turned off, so that it cools down with the oven. Then remove from the oven. Remove the lid and weight the terrine – but not too much, otherwise the jelly will push to the top, and it should remain all around the terrine.

Refrigerate overnight. The terrine should last a week or so. Serve with toast or crisp French bread.

Author's Note:

A time-consuming recipe but worth every second. You can use veal instead of rabbit, but it isn't as good. If you want a more 'gamey' terrine, use hare or venison.

Lalla says: 'This is my father's recipe and he's made it for all our parties for years and years to unanimous acclaim. I'm usually chief chopper and kitchen slave. It's hard work, but well worth the effort.'

Terry Molloy

Davros

Terry Molloy has appeared in major rep theatres throughout England. His many stage credits include *Under Milk Wood, Sweeney Todd, Circle of Glory, Pilgrim, The Mail Makers, Measure for Measure, Sherlock Holmes* and *Pinocchio.* He was the musical director for *Twelfth Night* and has also appeared in the tour of *Godspell, All Together Now, Triumph of Death, As You Like It, City Echoes* and many more.

He has appeared on TV in *God's Wonderful Railway, Angels, Carrot del Sol, Getting On* and *The Exercise.* Terry is also known for his radio work on such programmes as *The Archers, Afternoon Theatre, Beautiful City, Poor Pikeman* and *Risky City*, for which he won the 1981 Pye award for best actor.

Of course, Terry will always be remembered for his role in *Doctor Who* as Davros, the evil genius who created the Daleks.

Davros Dalek Dip

Serves 4 people

This dish is not for the squeamish or faint-hearted. Try it if you dare!

Davros has been known to suddenly change from what appears to be an outwardly quiet, reasonable, and very persuasive person to a screaming frothing banshee. I can't say what mood Davros was in when he so generously gave me his recipe as I received the recipe and ran. But backs to the walls, as they say, stiff upper lip, and here we go.

Ingredients:

2 smoked mackerel fillets
6 oz/171 g Philadelphia cream cheese
¾ small carton single (light) cream
½ tsp/¾ tsp/3 g salt
2 tbs/2½ tbs/38 ml lemon juice (or to taste)
1 tsp/1¼ tsp/7.5 g freshly ground black pepper (or to taste)
Paprika
Capers

Method:

Remove the skin from the mackerels, and flake the fish into a bowl. Make sure that all the bones have been removed. Add the Philadelphia cream cheese and the carton of cream, salt, pepper and the lemon juice.

Mash briskly with a fork or with an electric mixer. Whisk until a solid paste is achieved. Turn into individual portion bowls and decorate with a few capers, and a sprinkle of paprika. Place the bowls in a fridge to chill.

Serve with hot pitta bread or toast cut into strips.

Author's Note:

I have carefully studied this recipe as it is one that I personally know and have made myself. I can assure the readers that this dish is quite delicious. It is very moorish, and there is a great temptation to eat too much. (Maybe that is what Davros wants – *You have been warned!*)

Nabil Shaban

Sil in 'Vengeance on Varos'

Nabil was born in Amman, Jordan, on February 12, 1953, which makes him an Aquarian, a Dragon (according to Chinese Astrology) and a Thursday's Child. His paternal grandfather, a refugee from the Russian Revolution, claimed to be a descendant of Genghis Khan.

At the age of three because he had been born with an incurable disease rendering his bones dangerously fragile, he was sent to Britain where he has lived ever since. After a period of six years in Queen Mary's Hospital, Carshalton, Nabil went to the National Children's Home and School for the physically handicapped in Chipping Norton, Oxfordshire. Because his disease confined him to a wheelchair, the powers-that-be decreed that, on leaving school at the age of sixteen, he would work as a clerical assistant in a sheltered workshop for the disabled. Nabil, however, had other ideas.

Ten years later, with a diploma in business studies in one pocket and a degree in psychology and philosophy in the other, he began work with his friend Richard Tomlinson in creating the Graeae Theatre Company of performers with disabilities, and ever since 1980 has been acting and writing for the stage, film and television.

Sil's Slimy Slurp (Frogs' Legs in Seaweed Sauce)

Serves 2 people

Seaweed Sauce:
Ingredients:

1 oz/28 g butter
1 oz/28 g flour
¼ pt/5 oz/1½ dl milk
2 oz/56 g chopped mushrooms
4 oz/113 g purple seaweed, soaked for 30 minutes and drained
5 fl oz chicken stock (bouillon)

Method:
Put the milk, chicken stock and seaweed plus seasoning into pan and simmer for 20 minutes. Strain.

Melt butter in pan. Add flour, mix to smooth paste. Add milk etc. To paste *slowly*.

Fry mushrooms in butter. Add to sauce. Serve with Sautéed Frogs' legs.

Sautéed Frogs' Legs:
Ingredients:

4 pairs of frogs' legs
Milk to cover
1½ tsps/1¾ tsps/9 ml mixed herbs
½ tsp/¾ tsp/3 ml onion powder
White pepper
Flour
6 tbs/7½ tbs/114 ml butter

Method:
Soak frogs' legs in milk for 60 minutes. Remove from milk and sprinkle with mixed herbs, onion powder and pepper. Coat lightly with flour. Melt butter, and as soon as it sizzles, add the frogs' legs and sauté for 7 minutes on each side or until golden brown.

Remove to heated platter. Spoon butter from skillet over frogs' legs.

MAIN COURSES

FISH DISHES

Roger Delgado

The first Master

Roger Delgado first appeared in *Doctor Who* in 'Terror of the Autons' with his friend Jon Pertwee. He immediately became a cult with *Doctor Who* fans and the general public alike, as the greatest rival of the Doctor. This resulted in Roger appearing in many episodes of *Doctor Who*, as the Master, a renegade timelord bent on evil and destruction.

Roger Delgado was born on March 1, 1918 in London, during the last air raid of the 1914–1918 war. His full name was Roger Caesar Marius Bernard de Delgado Torres Castillo Roberto. The turning point in his life came when he walked out of a bank where he was working in the City of London in 1938 on a Friday and on the following Tuesday walked onto the stage of the Theatre Royal, Leicester to rehearse *You Can't Take it with You.* This performance resulted in him playing innumerable villains in all the media except cabaret and ice shows, his last well known villain being the Master.

In reality, Roger was one of the quietest and gentlest of men; he was very considerate of his fellow actors and I always remember him as a gentleman. I worked with Roger in the early sixties in a show called *Enrico* at the Piccadilly Theatre in London. Years later I was to recall what I thought to be fate or whatever you would like to call it, when at the dress rehearsal Roger made his entrance onto the stage and stood in a spotlight dressed in a black suit and tie. I shivered and didn't know why. Years later I was to see Roger, in an episode of *Doctor Who* dressed in the identical garb.

Tragically Roger was killed in a car crash in the South of France on the way to the set of a film. It is ironic that fast cars, a great passion of his, should have been the cause of his death.

Roger's widow, Kismet, has remarried but was willing to give me Roger's favourite recipe. He loved fish and this is the dish that Kismet used to make regularly for him. I have included this as a tribute to a fine actor and a beautiful person.

Salmon in Pastry

Serves 6 people

Ingredients:

2½lb/1133 g fresh salmon (skinned and boned)
3 oz/85 g butter
2 cloves of ginger in syrup (chopped into small pieces)
1 tb/1¼ tb/30 g currants (raisins)
Salt and pepper, to taste
1 lb/452 g puff pastry
1 egg

Method:
Mix the butter, salt and pepper, cloves of ginger, currants, all together and fill the cavity of the fish with the mixture. Roll out the pastry until it is thin and wrap the fish into it making a parcel. Then trim the edges and brush the pastry with egg yolk.

Bake for 30–35 minutes at 425°F, 220–230°C (Gas Mark 7 or 8).

Herb Sauce:
Ingredients:

2 shallots
1 tb/1 ¼ tb/30 g chervil and tarragon
2 oz/56 g butter
1 tsp/1 ¼ tsp/7.5 g plain flour
½ pt/10 oz/3 dl single (light) cream
Salt and pepper, to taste
1 tsp/1 ¼ tsp/7.5 g Dijon mustard
Lemon juice

Method:
Cook the shallots very gently until the onions are clear and soft but not brown. Next add the teaspoon of flour, ½ pint of cream, salt and pepper to taste and the teaspoon of Dijon Mustard. Cook very gently (in a double boiler if available; a pan will do, but be very careful not to burn) for approx. 10 minutes. Then beat in 2 egg yolks until the mixture thickens. Finally add a squeeze of lemon juice. Place the fish on a serving dish and put the sauce in a sauce boat for the guests to help themselves. The fish can be sliced into 6 portions.

Author's Note:
This is absolutely delicious. Another way of serving this dish is to cut the fish into portions and wrap each piece in the pastry, thereby letting the guest have his own individual portion.

Paul and Andrew Conrad

Romulus and Remus in 'The Twin Dilemma'

Paul and Andrew Conrad are identical twins. They often play jokes with teachers and friends alike by swapping places and generally helping to confuse everyone as to who is who. 'The Twin Dilemma' was the boys' first professional TV engagement, and as a result of being cast as Romulus and Remus they were the envy of their school. The two boys coped marvellously with the studio conditions and I know that they were quite sad when the story had been completed. I am happy to say that the two boys are back at school and studying hard for their examinations.

Andrew and Paul have given me their separate favourite main meals, and a joint dessert. Here for your 'Dilemma' is Remus's recipe.

Remus Pie

Serves 4 people

Ingredients:

8 oz/229 g smoked haddock (or any available smoked fish)
1 medium can of mushroom soup
1 packet plain potato crisps (chips)
Fresh tomatoes (sliced and skinned; enough to cover the dish)
Grated cheese

Method:
Cook the fish and then drain it. Flake the fish into pieces and add to the soup. Return to the heat and cook until the soup has properly heated. Then in the base of small individual bowls lay the fish and soup mixture. Place the peeled and sliced tomatoes on top then sprinkle very generously with the grated cheese and the crushed potato crisps. Place under the grill to brown, and serve immediately.

Author's Note:
This is a simple dish which would be very popular for that after-school snack, or a light snack during the evening while watching *Doctor Who* on TV.

Colin Baker

The sixth Doctor

Colin Baker was born in London. He then went to Manchester where he attended St Bede's School. On completing his schooling he trained to be a solicitor, and practiced for five years. He then decided to become an actor as he found that he enjoyed his performances in court.

He studied acting at the London Academy of Music and Arts. After leaving the Academy he toured around England in a production of *Plaintiff in a Pretty Hat* which was followed by a season at the Mermaid Theatre. Colin has appeared in repertory in Liverpool, Canterbury, Harrogate and Edinburgh and has also played at the Chichester Festival. He is very well known in Scandinavia where he has toured in several plays.

In 1984 he produced, directed and starred in a highly successful tour of Norway and Sweden in *The Mousetrap.* Colin's wife, Marion Wyatt, also appeared in the production. He has toured the UK in theatre presentations of *Flip Side*, *Underground*, *Odd Man In*, and *Doctor in the House.* Colin has also appeared in numerous pantomimes. He is best known for his numerous television appearances such as *Within These Walls*, *Road To Freedom*, *Public Eye*, *Villains*, *War and Peace*, *The Brothers* (in which he played the cult figure of Paul Merroney – a forerunner of J. R. Ewing), *For Maddy with Love*, *Dangerous Davies*, *Blake's Seven* and *Swallows and Amazons Forever.*

Colin has a wicked sense of humour, combined with enormous charm. However witty one tries to be, Colin's barbed wit can usually be relied upon to supply an even wittier retort. I think Colin will be the most interesting Doctor to appear in *Doctor Who.*

Here is a wonderful Swedish recipe from Colin that I have not had since I was last in Sweden.

Doctor's Temptation

Ingredients:

8 medium sized potatoes (thinly sliced and peeled)
2 large chopped onions
4 oz/113 g tin of anchovy fillets (or tuna fish)
5 fl oz/6 oz/1½ dl cream
2 oz/56 g breadcrumbs
1 oz/28 g butter
Seasoning to taste

Method:

Peel and slice the potatoes fairly thinly. Chop the onions. Lightly butter a suitable oven-proof dish; spread the onions and anchovy or tuna in a layer and cover with the sliced potatoes. (If you use a deep dish or large amounts of the ingredients, you can make several alternating layers. If so, the top layer should be potatoes.)

Pour the cream over evenly, sprinkle the breadcrumbs and dot with butter. Bake uncovered in a pre-heated oven 400°F, 200°C (Gas Mark 6) for about 50 minutes or until the potatoes are tender.

Author's Note:

This is not a dish for the diet conscious! It is delicious accompanied by a glass of chilled crisp dry white wine.

Anthony Ainley

The Master

Anthony Ainley was born on August 20 in London. He started work as an Insurance Clerk but decided to become an actor and so he enrolled at the Royal Academy of Dramatic Art. His stage experience is extensive and he has many TV credits to his name including work in London, New York, and Rome. His TV appearances include *It's Dark Outside*, *The Avengers*, *Whodunnit?*, *Spyders Web*, *Warship*, *The Pallisers*, *Nicholas Nickleby*, *Lillie* and *Upstairs Downstairs*. His films include *Oh What a Lovely War*, *The Land that Time Forgot*, *Inspector Clouseau*, *A Man for All Seasons*, and *The Devil's Claw*. He was educated in England and America and is the son of the famous actor, Henry Ainley.

Anthony's first appearance in *Doctor Who* was in 'The Keeper of Traken' as the ill-fated Tremas whose body was taken over by the Master. He has subsequently made a number of appearances as the arch villain, and I suspect that he will continue to make his dastardly appearances in the future.

I have known Anthony for a number of years, and, like the first Master, Roger Delgado, he is very gentle and quiet. The first time that we actually worked together was in the Tunbridge Wells Production of *Cinderella*, in 1982/3, when I taught Anthony to dance. He learned very quickly and showed a tremendous interest in the dance routines. In one number, 'Hey Look Me Over,' I surrounded him with eight lovely young ladies at the end of the number. I know Anthony enjoyed that part of the routine most of all.

I do enjoy telephoning Anthony. As the receiver is picked up one hears that famous voice saying, 'I am the Master, you will obey me.'

Anthony is very keen on that most English of English games cricket and plays every match he can. He is a member of the famous gentleman's club, the Garrick.

Anthony tells me he is not very good at cooking but the recipe he has given is one that he does cook himself. Here is Anthony's 'masterly' dish which I am sure you will enjoy.

A Master Prawn Curry

Ingredients:

½ lb/229 g fresh peeled prawns (shelled shrimps)
1 tin plum peeled tomatoes
1 large chopped onion
Salt and pepper, to taste
Curry powder, to taste
Handful of currants (raisins)
½ cup pineapple juice
1 banana
2 slices of pineapple
Selection of nuts
Mango chutney
½ cup Benedictine

Method:

Pour a tin of tomatoes into a medium-sized saucepan, and place on a slow heat. Add the chopped onion and mix with the tomatoes. Add the salt, pepper, and curry powder to taste. Throw in a handful of raisins. Stir together.

Pour in ½ a cup of pineapple juice. Gently plunge in the peeled prawns. Bring slowly to a gentle simmer for about 2½ minutes. Just before serving, add ½ cup of Benedictine to the curry and gently stir.

Chop up the banana and the two slices of pineapple with the selection of nuts to add with the Mango chutney when serving. This can be served with Pilau or plain rice, whichever is preferred.

Author's Note:

This dish is quick and simple to make and is very tasty. A chilled bottle of Sauvignon or iced lager would be ideal to accompany the Master Prawn Curry.

Nigel Stock

Professor Hayter in 'Time-Flight'

Nigel Stock was born on September 21, 1919 in Malta and wanted to be a doctor, a fact which has haunted him during his career in his many doctor roles. He played a medical student in *And No Birds Sing*, then he played Doctor Watson many times, the title role in *Owen M.D.*, which was one of Britain's most popular soap operas, and the same role in *The Doctors*.

He discovered that he liked acting by competing with his sister's party piece. He studied acting at RADA and acted until the Second World War. He served first with the London Irish Rifles and then the Assam Regiment in the Indian Army in Burma when he became a Major at twenty-three. He has made many stage and TV appearances including *Fall of Eagles*, *Churchill's People*, *On the Move*, *Wingate*, *London Assurance*, *Van Der Valk*, *Tinker, Tailor, Soldier, Spy*, *A Man called Intrepid*, and *Flesh and Blood*. He has made over forty films including *The Lion in Winter* and *Cromwell*.

Nigel is a very jolly man always ready for a practical joke and his humour is something to be experienced. I first worked with Nigel when I choreographed the *Cinderella* production at the Theatre Royal, Drury Lane, in 1973. Nigel and Jessie Matthews played the Duke and Duchess of Bookaroff and performed a parody of 'I Remember it Well' from the film *Gigi*. Also appearing were Peter O'Toole, Elaine Stritch, Judi Dench and many others. There were over 100 stars in the show.

I have known Nigel now for fifteen years and I never tire of listening to his fascinating anecdotes. Because he was in the East for a period, he loves spicy and hot dishes and has given a hot spinach and prawns dish which is simple to make. But stand by with your glasses of water!

Hot Spinach and Prawns

Serves 2 people

Ingredients:

1 lb/453 g prawns (shrimps)
1 packet green spinach
1 clove of garlic
1 onion
Crushed chilli peppers, to taste
Tabasco, to taste
Tomato purée (paste), to taste
Salt and pepper, to taste

Method:
Chop up the onion and garlic, and fry. Add the frozen spinach and cook until thawed. Add the prawns and the seasonings which can be as hot as you can take it. Heat through for 20–30 minutes and serve with saffron rice.

Author's Note:
The dish is a very handy meal for people who are busy and do not have a great deal of time. This is a perfect example of what I call a store cupboard meal – yet delicious all the same.

William Hartnell

The first Doctor

For many years William Hartnell learnt his trade as an actor in the provincial theatres around Great Britain, one of his first jobs being in a Shakespearean company. He did not break into movies until the 1930s when he was in great demand for various cameo roles. He played a variety of parts: village squires, petty criminals, killers, and the one that I remember most, an army sergeant. His big break came when he was cast in *This Sporting Life*, which brought him to the attention of Verity Lambert at the BBC who was casting for a new project, *Doctor Who*.

Playing *Doctor Who* meant instant success for Bill, and who knows how long he would have played the Doctor if illness had not robbed us of this very fine character actor? I never met William Hartnell, but I have had the pleasure of meeting and talking to his wife, Heather, his daughter, Ann, and his granddaughter, who is at the moment studying to become an actress. Heather was a very charming and lively lady, whose stories about her husband are absolutely fascinating.

Meddling Monkfish Chowder

Ingredients:

2 lb/906 g potatoes (peeled and diced)
3 or 4 large leeks (or 3 large onions)
2 lb/906 g monkfish (or any suitable local fish)
8 fresh scallops (or 1 lb/453 g frozen scallops)
1 lb/453 g Queen scallops
1 tin sweetcorn
1 pt/20 oz/6 dl milk
1 red pepper
½ lb/227 g peeled prawns (shelled shrimps)
Thyme
1 bay leaf
Oregano
Salt and black pepper
1 fresh lemon
1 cube fish stock (bouillon)
½ bottle of dry white wine (Heather prefers French)

Preparation:

Peel and dice the potatoes. Clean and slice the leeks (or onions) into slices. Skin and bone the fish then divide into bite size chunks. Dice the red pepper.

Method:

Put the potatoes and the leeks (or onions) into a fairly large pot, with just enough water (or fish stock) to cover the potatoes and leeks (or onions). Add the bay leaf and pinch of salt to taste, and simmer for 3 to 4 minutes.

Add the prepared monkfish together with the herbs (either a pinch or to taste) and wine. If there is too little liquid, add some of the milk. Simmer gently until the fish is tender. Prepare the fresh scallops by cutting the large ones into 3 or 4 pieces, cutting coral into 2 or 3 pieces if possible, and cutting the Queen scallops in half if necessary, and add to the pan, together with the sliced pepper, prawns, and the corn (having strained the liquid off). Flavour with black pepper, and add the rest of the milk. Simmer gently for not more than 4 minutes (or the scallops will become tough). Thicken the sauce if necessary with a little potato flour or instant mashed potatoes. (You may need to use a little extra milk.) Adjust the seasoning to taste.

This is delicious served with hot French Bread.

Author's Note:

This is an extremely lovely dish for those readers who enjoy fish. However do make sure that all the fish is fresh. An exotic dish but not for those with delicate stomachs.

John Scott Martin

John Scott Martin, known to generations of *Doctor Who* fans as the most evil monster of all, the Supreme Dalek, has fought his way through galactic battlegrounds with five different Doctors from Bill Hartnell through the Troughton, Pertwee, Baker and Davison eras.

John's career has also spanned many aspects of theatre. He was born in Liverpool where he studied singing and drama and has performed in Panto, Summer Shows, Musicals (spending two years in London's West End in *Oliver* and *The Streets of London*) and in films like *No Sex Please, We're British*, *The Wall* and recently Monty Python's *The Meaning of Life*. On TV John has been seen in many productions including *The Good Life*, *The Two Ronnies*, *Alice*, *The Pickwick Papers*, Classic Series like *The Forsyte Saga* and *The Pallisers*, and the childrens series *The Tripods*. His only human appearance in *Doctor Who* was as a Welsh miner in 'The Green Death', the story of the horrible green maggots. 'Jones the Maggot' they called him at rehearsal.

John lives far away from the hustle and bustle of space travel in a little village in North Essex called Great Maplestead. The children of the village know him as 'Mr Dalek', the man who is also the Church Warden and the guy who always seems to be organising daft games at village functions.

John is married and his wife, Margaret McKechnie, was for many years a singer in Pantos, Summer Shows and Cabaret. They have a daughter who is, of course, following in their footsteps and studying Drama and Music at Colchester College.

To keep themselves busy John and his wife have opened a Theatre Costume and Fancy Dress Hire business in nearby Sudbury. I bet their first customer wanted to hire a Dalek!

Dalek Bake with Exterminate Topping

Exterminates 4 humanoids

Ingredients:

1 lb/453 g white fish
4 oz/113 g fresh breadcrumbs
1 tsp/1¼ tsp/7.5 g salt
Pepper
1 tsp/1¼ tsp/7.5 g chopped parsley
2 beaten eggs
2 oz/56 g melted butter

Method:
Remove the skin and bones from the raw fish and chop it into small pieces. Mix it together with all the dry ingredients. Add the melted butter and beaten eggs. Press into a pudding bowl which has been greased and sprinkled with brown breadcrumbs.

Cover the bowl with a greased paper and bake in the oven for 45 minutes at 350°F, 180°C.

Topping Ingredients:

1 oz/28 g dripping
1 medium onion
½ oz/15 g curry powder
1 oz/28 g flour
½ pt/10 oz/3 dl stock (bouillon) or water
1 tomato (peeled and chopped)
1 dessertspoon lemon juice
1 dessertspoon plum or gooseberry jam (jelly)
1 grated carrot
Sugar
Salt

Method:
Melt the dripping and fry the onion and carrot. Sprinkle in the curry powder and flour and fry thoroughly. Gradually add in the stock until it begins to boil, then add the remaining ingredients and simmer for 45 minutes, with the lid on the pan.

To serve:
Turn the pudding on to a plate and into one side of the pudding stick two thin sticks of raw carrot. Attach a circle of gherkin to one stick. Either pour the hot topping over the pudding or serve in a separate dish or sauce-boat.

Author's Note:
What a novel way to make a fish pudding! I am sure children would love to try to cut into this and to exterminate it.

Faith Brown

Flast in 'Attack of the Cybermen'

Faith Brown was born in Liverpool in 1948. At one time she was a sales demonstrator at a Liverpool store. She started in showbusiness by entering a local talent contest and by the time she was sixteen she was singing in a Liverpool-based band.

When she went solo she began to do impressions and has since performed her act all over the world. Her TV credits include *Who Do You Do*, *For My Next Trick*, *Celebrity Squares*, *The Faith Brown Chat Show* and *Starburst*. She has also won the following TV awards: the Specialty Act of the Year Award in 1980, the *TV Times* Award for the Funniest Woman on TV in 1980, and the COPS (Californian Organisation of Police and Sheriffs) Award for her work for American charities.

Sole Suzanne

Serves 4 people

Ingredients:

6 fillets of sole
1 oz/28 g butter
Salt and pepper, to taste
Juice of 1 lemon
½ lb/250 g mushrooms
¾ pt/15 oz/4½ dl milk
1 tb/1¼ tb/30 g cornflour (cornstarch)
2 tbs/2½ tbs/38 ml double (heavy) or single (light) cream
Lemon slices
Black grapes
Water cress to garnish

Method:
Trim the fillets and roll them up. Place them in a lightly greased ovenproof dish. Dot with butter and season with salt and pepper. Sprinkle with lemon juice and bake in a moderate oven at 350°F, 180°C (Gas Mark 4) for 15 minutes.

Remove from the heat. Mix the cornflour with a little cold water and then stir in the mushrooms. Add a little more salt and pepper if needed, and a knob of butter. Add the cream and pour the mushroom sauce over the fish when cooked. Garnish with lemon slices, black grapes and watercress.

Author's Note:
This is not a very difficult dish to prepare at all and it certainly tastes wonderful! The combination of the mushroom sauce and the sweetness of the grapes complement each other wonderfully well.

Mat Irvine

Visual Effects Designer

Mat Irvine works as a Visual Effects Designer for BBC Television. Programmes he has been involved with include *Doctor Who, Blake's Seven, Moonbase Three, QED, Horizon, Tomorrow's World, The Sky at Night, Think of a Number, Medical Express, The Risk Business, Spaceships of the Mind, The Adventure Game, The Whole Universe Show, The Comet is Coming*, the Apollo/Soyuz Test Project coverage and the Space Shuttle coverage.

He has written many articles for a variety of publications, particularly the modelling magazine *Scale Models* and the film and television magazine *Starburst* and he was Technical Editor of *Voyager*. He has also contributed to the *Airfix Magazine, Hermes, Insight, Science Now*, and *The Beginner's Book of Astronomy*. His first book, a video book for children has recently been published and he is working on three more books on various subjects at present.

Mat has made regular appearances on *Saturday Superstore* and its predecessor *The Multi-Coloured Swap Shop*, talking on all aspects of effects work and space exploration. He has also appeared on *Pebble Mill at One*, the schools programme *Science Workshop, Tomorrow's World* and two modelling programmes. There have also been several radio interviews, including one for the British Forces network. He made a pilot *Mat and Mutt* story with K9, which was shown, on *Superstore* in early '84. He talks regularly to a wide range of societies and groups, including the British Interplanetary Society, the Model Engineering Exhibition, the British Association of Young Scientists, the Federation of Astronomical Societies, and has attended *Doctor Who, Blake's Seven* and *Star Trek* conventions.

Mat, who is a Fellow of the British Interplanetary Society, is 35, lives in Hertfordshire, and is fond of cats. He worked as Visual Effects Designer on 'The Face of Evil', 'The Stones of Blood', 'Warrior's Gate' and 'Warriors of the Deep', and as a Visual Effects Assistant in earlier years on 'The Curse of Peladon', 'Frontier in Space', 'Pyramids of Mars' and 'Planet of the Spiders'.

He was Visual Effects Designer for the one-off *K9 and Company*, where he also acted as K9's operator. He redesigned the mechanics of K9 for this last (mark 3) version, and has operated K9 in his other appearances on programmes such as *The Generation Game* and *The Computer Programme*. He also designed and built the infamous Boris the

Spider, initially for 'Planet of the Spiders'. Boris however has since become a star in his (or her) own right.

Pirate Paella

Of all the *Doctor Who* stories I've been involved with, my favourite has to be 'Warriors' Gate', which was different if nothing else! A large slice of the plot revolved around a motley bunch of space pirates who travelled the spaceways making a thorough nuisance of themselves in a dilapidated spaceship of dubious design and called, appropriately, *The Privateer.* Personally though I reckon a lot of the trouble, and most of the moans and grumbles, could have been avoided if the crew had treated themselves to a square (or any other shape for that matter) meal, and so I'm offering to the gallant lads ever-riding the Time Winds, a speciality left over from the Tharils' banquet – Pirate Paella!

Ideally this should be cooked in an appropriately shaped vessel, like the reflector dish of a discarded laser cannon, but for those of you restricted to more terrestrial apparatus, a large frying pan, wok or a paella itself is perfectly adequate.

Please note that Earth-bound cooks will have to use the alternative ingredients in brackets, unless they have access to an extremely versatile supermarket.

Serves 8 people

Ingredients:

1 small Arcturan sea lizard (squid) cut into small pieces
1 small Eta Carina cockerel (chicken), cut into small pieces
12 Theta Orionis sea snappers (mussels), fresh or tinned
3½ oz/100 g small Magellanic Cloud pinkitwisters (prawns/shrimps)
3 tbs/3¾ tbs/60 ml Hydroxoil (Olive or vegetable oil)
1 medium Manylayered Sagittarian fruit (onion)
2 Trapezium Tomatoes (Earth equivalents should be all right)
1 of each colour of Puppis Peppers (Earth cooks will be restricted to just red, green and yellow – shame)
3½ oz/100 g Cryogenic Pulses (frozen peas)
34 fl oz/4⅓ cups/1 litre Eta Carine cockerel liquor (chicken stock/bouillon)
Pinch of powdered stardust (saffron)
Sodium chloride (salt), to taste
Seyfert spice (pepper), to taste
10 oz/300 g long grain lunar lice (rice)
1 clove of garlic, which is the same in any solar system!

Method:

We will use the terrestrial equivalents for convenience. Pour the oil into whatever vessel you are using and fry the onion, peppers and garlic until soft, but not brown.

This usually takes about 300,000 nanoseconds (5 minutes). Add the chicken pieces and the tomatoes, and fry until the chicken is lightly browned. Stir in the stock and the rice, blend a little of the stock with the saffron and add this with the salt and pepper. Bring this to the boil and then simmer for 20–30 minutes, until most of the liquid has been absorbed and the rice is almost cooked. Add the squid, prawns, mussels and peas, and simmer for a further short time until all are heated and cooked.

Serve immediately. You will usually find that these proportions are enough for eight. If the crew of your Privateer has recently been on the rampage it might only just be enough for four, so adjust accordingly.

Bon Appetit!

Author's Note:

Well, I bet you never thought a recipe like this one would appear! Mat has been very inventive and this recipe is exactly as he wrote it. (I have included this recipe in the 'Fish Dishes' section as, despite the inclusion of chicken, fish is the dominant ingredient.) I would suggest a bottle of chilled Frascati to accompany this dish.

John Stratton

Shockeye o' the Quawncing Grig in 'The Two Doctors'

John Stratton was born on November 7, 1925 in Clitheroe, Lancashire. He was educated at the Royal Grammar School in Clitheroe and has appeared in rep in Dewsbury, Leeds and Hastings.

During the Second World War he served in the Royal Navy. After the war John appeared in rep in Dundee again before playing in the West End.

John made his first TV appearance in 1948, and since then he has never looked back, appearing in such productions as *Letters from the Dead, When we are Married, Forget Me Not, Backs to the Wall, Just William, Backs to the Land, Mill on the Floss, The Good Companions, Great Expectations, The Forgotten Story* and *The Tales of Beatrix Potter.*

His role in *Doctor Who* is out of this world and very appropriate for this book. It is exactly in tune with his character! John spent hours in full costume and make-up in the blazing hot Spanish sunshine in temperatures of around 110 degrees. He coped admirably and I rewarded him with cold beverages all day long and more especially back at the unit hotel at night.

His star sign is Scorpio, and his hobbies are Staffordshire pottery, tennis, and travel.

Coley Anorexique

An ancient British recipe, pre-empting *Cusine Minceur*

Ingredients:

1 lb/453 g Coley fillet (skinned by your obliging fishmonger; if he isn't obliging, change your fishmonger)
1 chopped Spanish onion (you have to do this yourself)
1¼ lb/556 g packet of petit pois
1 can of tomatoes
Salt, pepper and garlic to taste
½ glass dry white wine

Method:

Chop the Coley into substantial chunks, removing any bones which may have been left by your willing but harassed fishmonger.

Into a greased baking dish lay a layer of chopped onion, followed by the chunks of fish. Pour on the crushed tomatoes, mixed with the equally crushed garlic. Follow this with the frozen peas, and then the remaining chopped onions. Pour the half glass of wine into the dish, cover and place in a moderate oven, 350°F, 180°C (Gas Mark 4) for 40 minutes. Serve with boiled new potatoes, when in season, sprinkled with parsley.

You won't feel hungry again for at least two hours!

MEAT DISHES

Nicola Bryant

Companion to the fifth and sixth Doctors

Nicola Bryant is of British/American nationality. She studied at the Webber Douglas Academy of Dramatic Art, where she received a three year diploma; Nicola studied the flute, piano, and the guitar. She is also very proficient at dialects and accents. Her interest in sport includes swimming, tennis, netball and golf.

Nicola has also studied dance and is very good at classical ballet, modern ballet, jazz ballet and tap. *Doctor Who* fans in Chicago are well aware of Nicola's ability at tap as she and I performed a tap duet in cabaret at the huge convention in 1983 – 'The Ultimate Celebration'. The audience loved us. (Fred and Ginger eat your heart out!) Nicola's first recipe is a traditional hamburger dish.

Hamburgers in Mushroom Sauce

Serves 4 people

Ingredients:

1 lb/453 g lean minced beef
1 beef stock (bouillon) cube
1 chopped onion
1 tsp/1¼ tsp/7.5 g mixed herbs (or curry powder)
½ cup breadcrumbs
Oil
Salt and pepper
1 beaten egg

Sauce:
Ingredients:

2 oz/56 g chopped mushrooms
2 tsps/2½ tsps/38 ml horseradish sauce
1 oz/28 g grated Edam or Cheddar cheese (or similar)

Method:
Mix the meat, crumbled beef stock cube, onion, herbs, (or curry powder), breadcrumbs and salt and pepper. Bind the mixture with a beaten egg. Divide into 4 portions. Shape and fry in as little oil as possible for about 10 minutes on each side. Keep warm in a low oven. Fry the mushrooms in oil for about 1 minute. Stir in horseradish sauce and season with salt and pepper to taste. Spoon the sauce onto the hamburgers. Sprinkle with a little grated cheese. Return to a low oven so that the cheese can melt.

Author's Note:
The tangy sauce converts an ordinary hamburger into a masterpiece. You can serve it with watercress and tomatoes for extra vitamins.

Heather Hartnell

Beef Mustardis

Ingredients:

2 lb/906 g buttock steak
2 medium sized onions
2 or 3 fat cloves of garlic
4–6 oz/113–171 g mushrooms
Tumbler of red wine (*not* a cheap one, please!)
Cup of good stock (bouillon)
1 tb/1 ¼ tb/7.5 g mustard powder
Coriander
¼–½ pt/5–10 oz/1 ½–3 dl sour cream
Oil for frying

Method:

Cut the steak into ½ inch cubes or strips. Finely slice the onions, mushrooms and garlic. Gently fry the onions in oil for 2 to 3 minutes; add the crushed garlic, turn up the heat, and add the meat, having first removed all fat and any gristle. Fry quickly, turning after 2 or 3 minutes to brown both sides. Mix the mustard with a tablespoonful of water, and add to stock. Mix thoroughly, and add to pan with the wine, then cook at very high temperature for 3 or 4 minutes, to reduce the sauce. Add ½–1 teaspoonful of coriander, and at the last minute, stir in the sour cream.

Serve with mashed potatoes or on a bed of rice, with a green vegetable or salad.

Author's Note:

Another favourite of Bill Hartnell and after trying it, I can understand why.

Beef Mustardis can be eaten all year round, by just varying the supporting vegetables.

Peter Purves

Companion to the first Doctor

Peter Purves joined the cast of *Doctor Who* in 1965 playing the part of Steven Taylor, a marooned astronaut. He joined in the four-part serial 'The Chase', and stayed on in 'The Time Meddler', 'Galaxy Four', 'The Myth Makers', 'The Dalek Master Plan', 'The Massacre', 'The Ark', 'The Celestial Toyroom', 'The Gunfighters', and finally 'The Savages'. After Peter left the series he became the host of UK's longest running children's programme *Blue Peter*. He stayed there for several years.

Peter is now a very successful TV commentator, best-known perhaps for his coverage of darts. He is also the presenter of the sports programme, *Stopwatch*.

Peter is always busy with a variety of projects and lives near London. He has chosen a steak dish with a rather interesting sauce which I know you will love to try. So here is Peter's dish which he headed 'Doctor Ooh!'

Doctor Ooh's Fillet Steak

Ingredients:

4 good fillets of steak (or rump – as long as it has been beaten first)
3–4 tbs/3¾–4 tbs/90–120 g jellied beef of consomme
4 tomatoes (with seeds and peel removed)
2 oz/56 g butter
5 fl oz single (light) cream
1 medium sized onion, chopped into small pieces
1 small clove of garlic
Tomato purée (paste), to taste
1 glass medium sherry
Salt
Black pepper (freshly ground is best)
Chopped parsley as decoration

Method:

Melt the butter in a frying pan and then cook the steaks as you like them.

Remove the steaks from the pan, draining off the fat, and put them in a warmed dish (preferably with the lid on) to keep them hot enough to continue to cook.

Then cook the onion and the garlic together in the remaining butter until the onion is soft. Add the tomato flesh and let it all cook for a minute or two. Then, stirring all the time, add the sherry, the cream and the consommé. When mixed and well warmed, but not boiling, season to taste with the salt and the pepper and the tomato purée. Put the steaks on their individual plates which have been pre-warmed and pour the sauce over them. Decorate with the chopped parsley and serve.

Author's Note:

Doctor Ooh! So called because it is very rich.

The sauce is delicious. I make a similar sauce which an aunt of mine taught me how to make and we called it monkey gland sauce . . .

Mark Strickson

Turlough's Rolls

Serves 4 people

Ingredients:

8 thin slices of sirloin beef
8 thin slices of ham
4 cloves of garlic
8 thin slices of salami
4 oz/113 g raisins
2 oz/56 g Parmesan cheese
6 tbs/7½ tbs/120 g chopped parsley
Grated nutmeg
Grated oregano
Salt
Black pepper
1 bottle red wine

Method:

If not bought prepared, place each slice of beef between sheets of greaseproof paper and flatten with a rolling pin. Then cover the beef slices with a slice of ham and spread with crushed garlic. Finally chop the skinned salami into fine pieces and blend with the cheese, parsley, nutmeg and oregano. Add the salt and pepper to taste. Divide this equally over the beef and ham slices.

Fold over the long sides and roll up the slices. Tie the parcels with string. Place the rolls in a buttered ovenproof dish, and pour over the wine to cover them. Now leave them for at least two hours, preferably longer.

Pre-heat the oven to about 375°F, 190°C (Gas Mark 5) and cook for 45 minutes, or longer depending on how you like your beef cooked. Serve with a green salad, cold French green beans, with lemon juice and pepper over them, and plenty of garlic bread to mop up the delicious juices.

Author's Note:

Mark has given another dish which his wife, actress Julie Brennon cooked for me, and I heartily recommend it. It is an exotic-tasting dish which does take much preparation time, but it is well worth the effort.

Sarah Sutton

Nyssa – companion to the fourth and fifth Doctors

Sarah attended the Elmhurst Ballet School and the Bush Davies Ballet School. She started acting when she was nine years old, and lists among her credits Alice in BBC TV's *Alice through the Looking Glass*, *Oil Strike North*, *Late Call*, *Westway* and *The Moon Stallion*.

She has also performed in several radio plays and was Baby Roo in *Winnie the Pooh* for three seasons at the Phoenix Theatre, London.

Her interests include dancing, painting and travel. Sarah's first appearance in *Doctor Who* was in the eighteenth season in 'The Keeper of Traken'. She then appeared in the following stories: 'Logopolis', 'Castrovalva', 'Four to Doomsday', 'Kinda', 'The Visitation', 'Black Orchid' (in which she danced superbly), 'Earthshock', 'Time-Flight', 'Arc of Infinity', 'Snakedance', 'Mawdryn Undead', and 'Terminus'.

Sarah is a very good cook; I was invited to her twenty-first birthday party and she made a delicious dessert which appears later in this book. In the meantime Sarah has chosen to share with us her recipe for Lasagne.

Lasagne

Serves 4 people

Ingredients:

Enough lasagne for 4 people
1 onion peeled and sliced
1 lb/453 g minced beef
1 large tin of tomatoes
1 level tb/1¼ tb/19 ml tomato purée (paste)
Pinch of garlic salt
1 beef stock (bouillon) cube
1 Oxo cube
Salt and pepper
Butter or vegetable oil
½–¾ pt/10–15 oz/⅜ litre milk
2 tbs/2½ tbs/60 g plain flour
3–4 oz/85–113 g grated cheddar cheese (or similar)

Method:

In a large pan, fry the onion in the butter and a little vegetable oil until soft. Add the minced beef and fry until cooked right through. When the meat is all brown add the tomatoes, tomato purée, garlic salt, beef stock cube, Oxo cube and salt and pepper to taste. Simmer gently for about 20 minutes.

Meanwhile prepare the cheese sauce. Melt about 1–2 oz (28–56 g) of butter in a pan and add salt and pepper. Remove from the heat and mix in the plain flour. Return to the heat adding the milk a little at a time to form a smooth mixture.

Add 3–4 oz (85–113 g) of grated cheese until a smooth cheesey paste is made. Grease a large, deep oven-proof dish and arrange the meat sauce and cheese sauce in alternate layers with the sheets of pre-cooked spinach pasta, ending with a layer of cheese sauce. Sprinkle with a little remaining cheese and cook in an oven 350°F, 180°C (Gas Mark 4) for 45–60 minutes. Serve with a tossed green salad and, of course, a bottle of red wine, preferably Chianti.

Author's Note:

Italian food has always been one of my favourites. Do remember when making the sauce that it really is up to the individual how much or how few spices or herbs are added. I prefer lots of fresh garlic and an abundance of mixed herbs. This is perhaps why no-one comes too close to me after I've eaten Italian!

Nicholas Courtney

Steak Diane

Serves 6 people

Ingredients:

1½ lb/679 g best rump of beef
1 small onion
2 level tsps/2½ tsps/15 g caster sugar
1 large lemon
6 oz/168 g butter
Worcester sauce
1 level tb/1¼ tb/19 ml chopped parsley
4 tbs/5 tbs/76 ml brandy

Method:
Trim the steak and cut into six pieces. Beat them with a rolling pin until they are no more than an inch thick. Peel and finely chop the onion. Grate the lemon rind finely, squeeze the juice and strain.

Melt 2 oz (56 g) of butter in a large heavy-based pan and fry the onion for about 5 minutes or until it becomes soft and transparent. Lift the onion onto a plate with a perforated spoon and keep warm. Fry two steaks at a time over a high heat for 1 minute on each side. Keep them hot.

Melt another 2 oz (56 g) of butter until foaming and fry two more steaks, repeat with the remaining steaks. Return the onions to the pan and stir in sugar, lemon rind, and juice, add a few drops of Worcester sauce and parsley. Cook lightly then put in the steaks. Flame the steaks with warm brandy. Serve the steaks with onion and brandy poured over them. For vegetables I suggest new potatoes and braised celery.

Author's Note:
This famous dish is one of my favourites and originated in Australia where tender beef is obligatory. However rump steak is equally suitable. I suggest a lovely Beaujolais to accompany this dish. To be different, try chilling the wine: it tastes exquisite.

Fiona Cumming

Castrovalvan Kebabs

Ingredients:

1½ lb/679 g loin pork (chopped into cubes)
12 bay leaves
1 cup of white vinegar
2 tbs/2½ tbs/38 ml apricot jam (jelly)
½ bottle dry red wine
1 tb/1¼ tb/30 g sugar
1 tb/1¼ tb/30 g curry
1 tb/1¼ tb/30 g tumeric
1 lb/453 g sliced onions
2 crushed cloves of garlic
Salt and freshly ground pepper

Method:
Put the meat in a deep earthenware or enamel dish. Sprinkle with salt and pepper. Add the bay leaves, crushed garlic and sliced onions. Mix the curry, tumeric, sugar and jam in the vinegar and bring to the boil. Pour this mixture over the meat once it is cold. Lastly add the wine. Cover the dish and leave to marinate in the refrigerator for 2–3 days, stirring occasionally. When required, put the meat on skewers and grill on a barbeque. Baste with marinade and serve with plain boiled rice.

Author's Note:
Absolutely delicious. Fiona cooked this recently at one of her famous dinner parties, and it really was superb. A bottle of Beaujolais Village goes down very well with Castrovalvan Kebabs.

Ingrid Pitt

Zraza

Serves 4 people

Ingredients:

1½–2 lb/624–795 g sliced beef
2½ oz/65 g bacon (diced)
4 onions (diced)
Salt and black pepper
4 sour pickles (quartered)
Mustard
3–4 peppercorns
1 carton of soured cream
Butter
Some cornflour (cornstarch)
Water

Method:
Lay out the slices of beef on a board and flatten the slices with a meat tenderiser. Then spread a thin

coating of mustard over the slices and sprinkle salt and pepper over evenly. Put one or two pieces of pickle, a bit of diced bacon and onion at one end of the slice and roll up. Secure the roll with a toothpick or tie up with string (string is more secure). Put the rolls of beef into hot melted butter to brown evenly before cooking.

When the rolls of beef are nice and brown, take a pint of water (2½ cups 20 oz US) and stir into the brown butter on the bottom of the pot. This is after removing the meat rolls. When the broth is boiling add the Zraza, or meatballs and cook them for 1½ hours, making sure that the broth is simmering only. When adding the meatrolls add the salt and peppercorns as well. When the Zraza are cooked, remove from the pot and place in a warm oven while cooking the sauce as follows. Mix the cornflour with the water and stir into the broth of the Zraza. Let it come to the boil and thicken. Then fold in the sour cream and salt to taste. Put the Zraza back into the sauce and serve.

Author's Note:
Zraza is otherwise known as Russian Meat Rolls. I think a bottle of California Red Joseph Phelps Cabernet Sauvignon 1978, or a lovely bottle of Nuit-St Georges, les Maladière 1980 would go well with this dish.

Peter Moffatt's red cabbage would make a delicious accompaniment to Ingrid's Zraza.

Brian Hodgson

Radiophonic Workshop

Brian Hodgson, born in Liverpool and an ex-actor, joined the BBC in 1960 and the Radiophonic Workshop in 1962. In 1963 he was asked to create the sounds and voice treatments for a new series called *Doctor Who*. He was responsible for all the special sounds and voice treatments until 1972 when he left the BBC and spent a happy five years setting up Electrophon Music, producing records with his partner, John Lewis, and writing film and ballet scores including *Legend of Hell House*, part of *Visions of Eight*, *There was a Time*, *Weekend and Duets* for the Ballet Rambert and *Forest and Field* for the London Contemporary Ballet Company.

He returned to the BBC in 1977 as Organiser of the Radiophonic Workshop and became its Head in August 1983.

Gammon Gallifrey

Serves 4 people

Ingredients:

4 × ½ in/1¼ cm thick slices raw gammon
4 cloves of garlic
2 oz/56 g butter
1 tin of pineapple rings and juice

Method:
Into a small casserole dish, about the size of the gammon slice place 1 pineapple ring. In the centre of the ring place ½ oz butter and 1 crushed garlic clove. Cover with a slice of gammon. Repeat until all the gammon is in the casserole and a ring of pineapple has covered it. Then add the juice of the pineapple and cover.

Bake in a moderate oven until gammon is tender. Discard juice and serve.

Author's Note:
A very simple but tasty dish. Serve with vegetables of your choice. I personally like to have mashed potatoes with lots of butter and pepper and petit pois with this dish.

Lynda Baron

Wrack in 'Enlightenment'

Lynda Baron became well known to millions of viewers on TV as Nurse Gladys Emmanuel in the top-rated BBC TV comedy series *Open All Hours*, starring Ronnie Barker.

Lynda originally made her name in the West End of London in a revue called *One Over the Eight* with Kenneth Williams. She then worked extensively in cabaret in London working with that well-known female impersonator Danny La Rue. For two years she was the leading lady at London's famous nightclub, the Talk of the Town, before moving on to work at the famous Pigalle Theatre-Restaurant.

I met Lynda during this period and she is truly marvellous. She is one of the most dynamic artistes that I have ever seen. Since then Lynda has worked regularly on stage and in television and has undertaken many National Tours. She also regularly plays Principal Boy in pantomimes such as *Aladdin*, *Sleeping Beauty*, *Robin Hood*, and *Jack and the Beanstalk*.

Lynda's other theatrical credits include *The Bedwinner*, *A Bedful of Foreigners*, *Not Now, Darling*, *Irma La Douce*, *Move Over Mrs Markham*, *Butterflies are Free*, and *Key for Two*.

One of Lynda's first television appearances was on *That Was the Week that Was* with David Frost, and she has returned to the small screen on numerous occasions to appear in such series as *Z-Cars*, *Breaking Point*, *Don't Forget to Write* (on which I worked as Assistant Floor Manager), *Men of Affairs*, *Roof Over my Head*, *Oh No, it's Selwyn Froggitt*, *Grundy Heartlands*, *Minder*, and, of course, *Doctor Who* when she played the part of Captain Wrack.

Recently Lynda recreated the character of 'Lily Bless Her' in another long running TV series, *Last of the Summer Wine*. In 1984 she returned to the West End to co-star with Russ Abbot in the successful revival of *Little Me*. Her husband John and daughter Sarah and I have been friends for many years. Sarah is well known to *Doctor Who* fans as she is the personal secretary to the current producer of *Doctor Who*, John Nathan-Turner.

Here is Lynda's amusing dish, very English and very traditional.

Wrack of Lamb

Serves 6 Ephemerals or 3 Eternals

Ingredients:

Best end of neck of lamb (6 cutlets)
Salt and pepper
Rosemary, or mint sauce, mint jelly or redcurrant jelly

Method:

Have the backbone sawn off by the butcher (unless you like sawing things up yourself – Wrack does), and simmer the bone with an onion to make gravy stock. Crack the end bones about 4 inches down the bone so that they fold under the joint. Remove the skin from the top of the joint. Wipe dry and put in a roasting tin with the end bones tucked well under to make a neat joint. Put a little fat in the roasting tin. Here you have a choice of seasoning: a) sprinkle liberally with rosemary; or b) glaze the top with mint sauce or jelly; or c) glaze the top with redcurrant jelly.

Then cover the joint of meat with tinfoil (aluminium foil) and cook for about 1½ hours in a pre-heated oven 350°F, 180°C (Gas Mark 4). 15 minutes before the end of roasting time remove the foil from the joint, sprinkle with salt and pepper to taste, and baste. Then finish cooking the joint without covering so that the top is a rich golden brown colour. Serve with roast potatoes, French green beans, and broccoli.

Author's Note:

This traditional English Sunday lunch can be served at any time of the year. I prefer red wine with this dish. I do hope you have fun making the Captain's Wrack of lamb.

Opposite: Across time and space Colin Baker offers just what the Doctor ordered!

Overleaf: Packing a punch is the Doctor's lovely American assistant, Peri (Nicola Bryant)

STUNTS
Nobody
Does
it
Better

Terry Molloy

Davros's Ribs of Revenge

Serves 4 people

Ingredients:

3 lb/1359 g pork spare ribs
2 oz/56 g butter
1 large diced onion
1 crushed clove of garlic
4 tbs/5 tbs/120 g brown sugar
4 tbs/5 tbs/76 ml Worcester sauce
4 tbs/5 tbs/76 ml tomato purée (paste)
1 cup of beef stock (bouillon)
½ tsp/¾ tsp/3 g black pepper
1 tsp/1¼ tsp/7.5 g mustard
½ tsp/¾ tsp/3 g dried sage

Method:
Pre-heat the oven to 375–400°F, 190–200°C (Gas Mark 5–6) and place the spare ribs on a wire mesh rack in a roasting tray.

Melt the butter in a large pan until the foam subsides, then add the onion, garlic, salt and pepper and cook until soft. Add the brown sugar, Worcester sauce, tomato purée, beef stock, mustard and sage, and cook on a high heat for 2 minutes, stirring constantly.

Simmer for about 5 minutes. Pour the sauce over the spare ribs, making sure that they are coated all over and place in the centre of the oven for about one hour. Baste the ribs every 15 minutes. Serve with a fresh mixed salad.

Author's Note:
One of my favourite dishes. This particular recipe is delicious.

Previous page: A mouth-watering delicacy from 'Planet of Fire' director, Fiona Cumming

Opposite: Nobody does it better in the kitchen than Jamie McCrimmon (Frazer Hines)!

Nerys Hughes

'Todd' in the Hole

Serves 4 people

Ingredients:

4 oz/113 g plain flour
½ tsp/¾ tsp/3 ml salt
1 egg
½ pt/10 oz/3 dl milk
1 lb/453 g skinless sausages

Method:
Sift the flour and salt into a bowl. Add the egg and half the milk. Gradually stir in the flour and beat until it becomes smooth. Add the remaining milk, while continuing to stir the mixture. Put the sausages into a shallow ovenproof dish or Yorkshire Pudding tin and pour in the batter. Then place in an oven and bake for 40–45 minutes at 425°F, 220°C (Gas Mark 7), or until the batter is well risen and golden brown.

Author's Note:
Everyone has heard of Toad in the Hole, amusingly called 'Todd' in the Hole here by Nerys, in memory of the character, she played in *Doctor Who*.

I find this dish to be a good stand-by if unexpected guests arrive. It is best served with seasonal vegetables of one's own choice, and lots of hot gravy.

Robert Holmes

Writer

Robert Holmes was born in Hertfordshire in 1928. He started earning a living as a journalist and after enjoying a successful career in this vein he started writing for TV in 1960.

Robert Holmes has written more *Doctor Who* scripts than any other writer. He was the script editor on the show for four years, while Phillip Hinchcliffe was producing. He started writing with the Troughton series and has continued up to the present day with the sixth Doctor, Colin Baker. Robert is a grandfather, so he is very experienced at scaring children. He has written for *Coronation Street*, *Bergerac*, *Emergency Ward Ten*, and *Doctor Finlay's Casebook*. His science-fiction credits include *Undermind* for Thames TV, and *Doomwatch*, *Blake's Seven* and *Doctor Who* for BBC TV.

Here is Robert Holmes's recipe. It is accompanied by a short story.

Corned Beef Hash

Serves 4 people

My favourite accompaniment to *Doctor Who*, when shown on a Saturday evening, is toast with Marmite or Gentlemen's Relish. This hash is second favourite and is almost as easy to prepare.

It is an American version of Pan Haggerty and, I like to imagine, was invented by lumberjacks in Oregon. It is the sort of thing you need when chopping down Ponderosa pines. Almost all children seem to like it, perhaps because it can be forked down without losing an eye-flicker of screen-time. My own offspring, their appetites no whit diminished, charmingly referred to it as 'dog-sick'!

Bed-sitting students may also be attracted by this recipe because it is filling, fairly economical, and can be made on a single ring.

Ingredients:

1 lb/453 g potatoes
11 oz/314 g can of corned beef
1 can of sweetcorn
½ green pepper
1 medium sized onion
2 oz/56 g butter
1 tb/1¼ tb/30 g flour
1 chicken stock (bouillon) cube
Salt and pepper
Worcester sauce (optional)
Cooking oil, lard or butter

Method:

Peel and dice the potatoes. Seed the pepper and chop it up with the onion. You can now boil this lot together in one pan. Open the corned beef (if the thing on the side breaks off half-way round, as it usually does, get out the trusty sonic screwdriver), and dice the meat. Drain off the sweetcorn. Melt the butter, add the flour and stock and stir until you have a smooth sauce. Mix the vegetables and meat with the sauce. Heat your oil in a heavy frying pan. When sizzling, add the mixture, stir in the seasoning plus, if you wish, a dash or two of Worcester Sauce. Smooth the surface and turn down the heat to simmer. After six or seven minutes the hash should begin to turn crisp and brown underneath.

Serve with green salad or, damn the carbohydrates, a hunk of garlic bread.

Author's Note:

A recipe that a lot of readers with children might find useful. Excellent as an after-school snack.

Terrance Dicks

Writer

Terrance was born in East Ham, London and educated at East Ham Grammar School and Downing College, Cambridge. After two years national service in the army, he began work as an advertising copywriter and worked in advertising for about five years.

Towards the end of this time he began selling scripts, starting with a couple of radio plays and a comedy series. This led eventually to a career as a freelance script writer and this in turn led to the offer of the job of script editor of *Doctor Who*.

Terrance worked on *Doctor Who* for about six years, working on the last few Patrick Troughton shows and script-editing the shows for the whole of Jon Pertwee's time as the Doctor.

He left the show at the same time as Jon Pertwee and returned to being a freelance writer. At about this time, the *Doctor Who* novelisation programme took off and over the next few years he became increasingly involved in this. He has now written more than fifty *Doctor Who* books for Target. This led to the writing of other children's books, including *The Baker Street Irregulars* – a series of detective stories; *Star Quest* – a science-fiction trilogy; a series of six children's horror novels published by Blackie; plus a number of books for younger readers – the *Ask Oliver* and *David and Goliath* series.

At the moment Terrance is at the BBC, script editing the BBC 1 Classic Serial, and working with Barry Letts, who was his producer on *Doctor Who*.

Shobogan Stew

Legend has it that during his younger days the Doctor attracted considerable disfavour from his teachers at the Academy because of his taste for roaming the remoter areas on Gallifrey, and associating with companions quite unsuitable to his rank.

During his wanderings, he became very fond of this simple but filling dish which is a favourite of the planet's less reputable classes.

Ingredients:

Long grain rice (enough for each guest)
Tomatoes, onions and any vegetables
Any scraps of meat available

Method:

Boil water in a large cauldron and throw in a handful or two of long-grain rice for each member of the company. Cook for about 20 minutes, until the rice is firm but not soggy, and the water boiled away.

Meanwhile, in another small pot, boil up a savoury mess of tomatoes, onions, and any scraps of meat that may be available. When the guests are assembled, empty the contents of the pot into the cauldron, and issue spoons.

Home-brewed Old Gallifreyan Ale should be served with this dish, the more the better, as it helps to disguise the taste. At the end of the feast, it is customary for those members of the company still conscious to present their compliments to the chef.

Author's Note:

Use any left-overs from the Sunday joint as the meat base. I would add a bit of zest to this by adding a glass of red wine and a teaspoon of mixed herbs to heighten the flavour a little.

Johnny Byrne

Spiced Rib of Baanjxx

Baanjxx – the elusive arboreal browser native to Gallifrey – feeds exclusively on the truffle-flavoured nut of the cerub tree. Over-indulgence in this volatile nut induces an hallucinogenic frenzy which transforms this normally docile animal into a destructive juggernaut. Many blame the Doctor's ofttimes eccentricities on the fact that he was once kicked in the head by a rampaging Baanjxx.

Ingredients:

1 Baanjxx (if no Baanjxx is available use prime rib of beef on the bone) (about 6–8 lb/171–228 g)
1 tb/1 1/4 tb/30 g dry mustard
Freshly ground black pepper
1 crushed clove of garlic
1 tsp/1 1/4 tsp/7.5 g ground spice
3 oz/85 g softened butter
Salt, to taste

Method:

Pre-heat the oven to 425°F, 218°C (Gas Mark 7).

Blend all the dry ingredients plus the crushed garlic into the butter, and spread over the beef. Place the beef on a rack over a roasting pan and brown in the oven for 20 minutes. Reduce the heat of the oven to 390°F, 200°C (Gas Mark 5) and continue to roast, basting frequently, allowing 15–18 minutes per pound for rare beef, or 20–25 minutes for well-done beef.

When the beef is cooked, season with salt to taste, and transfer to a warm serving plate and stand for 15–20 minutes at the edge of the oven before carving. This enables the beef to set, thus facilitating carving. Serve with mixed salad or a vegetable of your own choice.

Author's Note:

This recipe is used regularly in the Byrne household. Sandi, Johnny's glamorous wife, devised it and the baby Byrnes enjoy it as much as Ma and Pa.

Peter Moffatt

Director of 'State of Decay', 'The Visitation', 'Mawdryn Undead', 'The Five Doctors', 'The Twin Dilemma', 'The Two Doctors'

Peter Moffatt was educated at Bootham School in York, England and trained as an actor at the St John School of Music and Drama in Newcastle. During the Second World War he served as an RAF Navigator in the Bomber Command. From 1943 until 1945 he was a prisoner of war, during which time he worked in the Prison Camp Theatre as an actor and director.

After the war, Peter started acting at the Colchester Repertory Theatre. He then went on to appear in most of the major repertory theatres throughout England and Scotland. At the same time he wrote a number of revues which were performed in the theatre and on television. Peter also appeared in the West End of London in a number of productions as an actor and stage manager/understudy.

He started training as a director for TV in 1959, and since then has become one of the most successful TV directors in British television, working for all the major TV companies in England, Scotland and Wales.

In recent years he has spent most of the time with the BBC, working on shows such as *Juliet Bravo*, *The Camerons*, *All Creatures Great and Small*, for BBC TV and, of course, *Doctor Who*. I first met Peter when I worked with him on *All Creatures Great and Small* as an Assistant Floor Manager. I worked again with Peter on 'The Two Doctors' which we filmed partly on location in Spain.

Peter is married to director Joan Kemp-Walsh, and lives in a beautiful London mews house. He has given a delicious Greek dish as he and his wife love taking their holidays in the Greek Islands.

Mouffatta's Moussaka

Ingredients:

3 or 4 medium sized aubergines (eggplants)
Juice of 1 lemon
2 onions
1 oz/25 g butter
1 lb/450 g lamb or veal (minced)
1 tsp/1¼ tsp/7.5 g ground cinnamon
2 tbs/2½ tbs/30 ml tomato purée (paste)
3 tbs/3¾ tbs/45 ml red wine
3 tbs/3¾ tbs/45 ml water
Handful of chopped parsley
Pinch of dried basil or oregano
4 oz/113 g thinly sliced Gruyère cheese
Salt and black pepper

For the Topping:

Grated Parmesan or Cheddar cheese
2 oz/56 g butter or margarine
2 oz/56 g plain flour
¾ pt/15 oz/450 ml milk
A little grated nutmeg
2 eggs
2 tbs/2½ tbs/38 ml single (light) cream
Salt and black pepper

Method:
Peel and slice the aubergines. Smear them with the lemon juice to prevent discolouration. Sprinkle with salt and leave to drain in a colander to remove bitterness. Peel and chop the onions and sauté in the butter in a large frying pan until brown.

Add the mince, turning and mixing it with the onions until it is browned all over. Add the cinnamon, the salt and pepper, the tomato purée, wine and water.

Stirring all together bubble over a higher heat until the moisture is absorbed. Turn off the heat and add the finely chopped parsley and herbs.

Add the aubergine slices to a large pan of boiling water, cover the pan and boil for 2 minutes. Drain and rinse under cold water. Lightly grease the bottom of a wide ovenproof dish, about 3 inches deep, with butter paper then cover with a layer of aubergine slices. Cover this with a few slices of Gruyère cheese, then the mince mixture, and finish with a layer of aubergine slices. Place in a moderate oven and cook for 30–45 minutes at 350°F, 180°C (Gas Mark 4).

The Topping:
Melt the butter in a saucepan, remove from the heat and stir in the flour. Then stir in the milk, gradually at first and bring to the boil stirring continually, and bubble gently, continuing stirring for about three minutes. Season lightly with salt and pepper and a little grated nutmeg. Remove from the heat. Whisk the eggs with the cream and add to the white sauce, mixing thoroughly. Cover the aubergine and mince layers and sprinkle with grated cheese. Return to the oven, and cook for a further 30 minutes or until the dish is a rich golden brown on top. Cut into slabs to serve.

Author's Note:
Moussaka is often running in fat, and the secret of this recipe is that the aubergines are not fried as in the usual method, but briefly boiled instead. It can be made with minced beef, but is much nicer if made with lamb or veal. This is a lovely Greek dish which is complemented by Retsina.

John Stratton

Shockeye Moussaka

Serves 4 diet conscious people

Ingredients:

1 lb/453 g lean cooked lamb
2 medium onions
1 can of crushed tomatoes (or 1 can of tomatoes without the juice)
3 courgettes (zucchini)
5 oz/143 g grated Cheddar cheese (or similar)
1 clove of garlic – or more, if you prefer!

Method:
Mince together the lamb and the onions. Add tomatoes, and season with salt, pepper, and garlic.

Place the sliced courgettes in a saucepan, and pour on boiling water. Simmer for about 6 minutes until they are cooked but still firm.

Take a greased dish, and lay alternate layers of the meat mixture with layers of courgettes together with the grated cheese. Finish off with a layer of courgettes and finally a layer of cheese.

Bake in a moderate oven, 350°F, 180°C (Gas Mark 4) for 1 hour.

Author's Note:
This is another version of Moussaka for you to try. It is really delicious, and goes well with a green or mixed salad.

Sarah Hellings

Director of 'The Mark of the Rani'

Having trained as a BBC film editor, Sarah got an interview for her first directing job because she'd listed pistol-shooting as one of her hobbies! (She has shot for Oxford University.) For several years she directed films for *Blue Peter* in locations varying from the Bishop Rock Lighthouse to the Amazon River. Sarah is now a freelance director and as well as *Doctor Who* she has directed *Grange Hill*, *Angels*, *Juliet Bravo*, and a play for BBC 2, *The World Walk*.

Her hobbies now include cooking, gardening, her film cameraman husband and their two cats.

Rani Steak Casserole

Serves 4 people

Ingredients:

2 lb/906 g piece of topside, cut into large strips
1 dessertspoon sugar
2 tbs/2½ tbs/60 g flour
3 onions
1 large clove of garlic
1 tb/1¼ tb/19 ml Worcester sauce
2–3 rashers (slices) of streaky bacon
2 tbs/2½ tbs/38 ml tomato purée (paste)
2 tbs/2½ tbs/38 ml vinegar
¼ pt/5 oz/1½ dl stock (bouillon)

Method:

Coat the meat pieces with flour and sugar. Line an ovenproof dish with two thinly sliced onions. Sprinkle with garlic and put meat on top. Pour sauces over. Stand 24 hours in a cool place.

When ready to cook, top with the remaining onion, cut into rings, and the bacon, cut into large pieces. Cook covered at 350°F, 180°C (Gas Mark 4) for 2–2½ hours. Take lid off for final 20 minutes of cooking time to crisp up top. Serve with hot French bread or new potatoes, and green salad.

Author's Note:

Absolutely delicious, especially with a bottle of Puis Flusse (or even two).

POULTRY AND GAME

Waris Hussein

Director of 'An Unearthly Child'

Waris Hussein was born in Lucknow in India, on December 9. He is one of Englands' foremost film and TV directors. His TV credits include *Wednesday Plays*, *Sleeping Dog*, *Death of a Teddy Bear*, *Toggle*, and *Spoilt Days in the Trees*. He then directed the following Plays of the Month: *A Passage to India*, *Girls in Uniform* and *St Joan*. He directed TV's *Casual Affair*, then directed the films *A Touch of Love*, *Quackser*, and *Fortune Has a Cousin in the Bronx*.

He spends most of his time living in California, and travels to London whenever he is able to get away from the rigours of work.

Waris has given one of his mother's recipes from his home town in Lucknow in India, which he has told me is one of his most favourite recipes.

Lucknow Spiced Chicken

Ingredients:

1 × 3 lb/1359 g chicken
5 large tomatoes
1 large onion
6 cloves of garlic
1 tsp/1 ¼ tsp/7.5 g tumeric
2 oz/56 g cooking fat
1 tsp/1 ¼ tsp/7.5 g cummin
1 tsp/1 ¼ tsp/7.5 g garam marsala
½ tsp/¾ tsp/3 g salt
1 tsp/1 ¼ tsp/7.5 g caster sugar
½ tsp/¾ tsp/3 g ginger

Method:

Wash and clean and joint the chicken, and fork it well. Skin and chop the tomatoes. Mince the onion and garlic and add the tumeric, cummin, garam marsala, ginger, sugar and salt. Rub the mixture well into the chicken and let the pieces soak in the spice for at least 2 hours.

Then heat the fat in an enamel casserole dish, and put in the chicken with the spices and add the tomatoes. Cover and put in a pre-heated moderate oven (350°F, 177–180°C, Gas Mark 4) till the chicken is soft and tender. Then remove to the top of the stove, uncover the dish and fry on a gentle heat till the spices and gravy are dry. Stir often so that the chicken pieces do not stick to the pan or burn.

Author's Note:

This dish could be served with the traditional rice, or with a green salad. Iced lager served with this is ideal.

Leonard Sachs

Lord President Borusa in 'Arc of Infinity'

Leonard Sachs was born on September 26, 1909, in Roodeport Transvaal, South Africa. He was educated at the Jeppe High School, Johannesburg, and then went to the Witwatersrand University.

His first appearance on the stage was in 1926 in South Africa and three years later, he appeared on stage in London. He has a wide theatre experience both as an actor and director.

In 1936, together with Peter Ridgeway, he founded the famous Players Theatre, and except for his army service, he directed and produced at the Players until 1947. He is probably best known for his role as the Chairman of BBC TV's *The Good Old Days* which ran for thirty years. His other TV appearances have been in *Family at War*, *Coronation Street*, *The Man from Haven*, *Crown Court*, and *The Glittering Prizes*. He is married to actress Eleanor Summerfield and has two sons, Robin and Toby.

His star sign is Libra and his hobbies are walking and swimming. His best known part in *Doctor Who* was as President Borusa in 'Arc of Infinity', where he played alongside Peter Davison, but he also took the part of the Admiral de Coligny in the 1966 adventure, 'The Massacre'.

Duck à l'Orange

Serves 4 people

Ingredients:

1 fresh duckling
Bouquet Garni
4 oranges
1 oz/28 g butter
2 oz/56 g plain flour
1 tb/1¼ tb/19 ml tomato purée (paste)
1 tb/1¼ tb/19 ml redcurrant jelly
½ pt/10 oz/3 dl stock (bouillon)
¼ pt/5 oz/⅛ litre red wine
2 tb/2½ tbs/38 ml brandy
1 bay leaf

Method:

Wash the neck and giblets, then simmer for 1 hour with the bouquet garni to make the stock. Joint the duckling with a sharp knife and prick the skin lightly with a fork.

Grate the rind from 2 oranges. Melt the butter in a pan and fry the duck pieces until golden brown all over. Remove the duck and place in a casserole. Add the grated rind to the butter and cook for 2 minutes. Stir in flour until smooth and cook gently for 2 minutes, then add the tomato purée, redcurrant jelly, wine, brandy, stock, the strained juice of 2 oranges and the bay leaf. Stir over a gentle heat to make a smooth sauce. Season to taste and pour over the duck in the casserole. Cover and cook in a slow oven 300°F, 150°C (Gas Mark 2) for 2–2½ hours until tender.

Ten minutes before serving skim off the excess fat. Peel the remaining oranges, divide into segments and add to the casserole. If you want a touch of green add some fresh garden peas.

Author's Note:

Another excellent recipe, for those special occasions.

Jackie Lane

Dodo – companion to the first Doctor

Jackie Lane was born and raised in New York under her proper name of Jocelyn Lane, but changed it to Jackie for her role in *Doctor Who*.

Her major film appearances were in *Men of Sherword Forest*, *The Gamma People*, *Tickle Me*, *The Sword of Ali Baba*, *Incident at Phantom Hill*, and *Land Raiders*.

She arrived in England in the 1950s and returned to America in the 1960s, returning once more to England when she landed the part of Dodo. Her first appearance in *Doctor Who* was in 'The Massacre', and her last was in 'The War Machines', making a total of six stories.

Jackie Lane is now part of one of London's foremost agencies dealing in voice-overs for TV commercials, handling, among others the fourth Doctor, Tom Baker.

Jackie has chosen a very tasty chicken dish for two or more people. One chicken is enough for four people, but you will need more than one for larger gatherings. The recipe can be adapted for two people by using chicken joints.

The amounts of the ingredients are to your own taste for as Jackie told me, 'The trouble with my cooking is that it is mainly guesswork as far as amounts go.' I do hope you enjoy experimenting with this dish.

Chicken Chaplet à la Dodo

Ingredients:

1 chicken large enough for 4 people
Juice of 1 lemon
Juice of 1 orange
1 tb/1 1/4 tb/30 g coriander seeds
1 cupful mixed currants and sultanas
3 oz/85 g chopped walnuts
2 small cartons of natural yoghurt
Rice for 4 people

Method:

Heat the lemon, orange juice and a cupful of water with the coriander seeds. Spread a little fat over the chicken to allow to brown and roast it in the juices and coriander, basting it from time to time.

When the chicken is nearly ready, boil the rice. Drain and separate. Add the dried fruit, nuts and yoghurt to the rice. Mix thoroughly and pour over a little of the juice from the chicken. Return to oven to heat through. Roughly carve the chicken and arrange in the centre of the serving dish. Spoon over a little of the juices. Surround the chicken with the heated rice mixture and serve either with broccoli or a green salad.

Author's Note:

Jackie says that she prefers this dish with plain rice but the combination of dried fruit and nuts gives it a more exotic look. With the fruit and nuts I think this dish is sheer delight.

Maurice Denham

Professor Edgeworth/Azmael in 'The Twin Dilemma'

Maurice Denham celebrated fifty years in showbusiness in 1984! He was born on December 23, 1909, in Beckenham, Kent and was educated in the charming town of Tonbridge. Maurice made his stage debut in 1933 and from then until 1940 he had an extensive stage career. In 1940 he joined the army, and on being demobilised in 1946 he made his first movie in *Home and School*, followed by *Daybreak*, *The Man Within*, *Take My Life*, *The Upturned Glass* and many others. His massive list of TV credits include *Porridge*, *Marie Curie*, *The Upchat Line*, *Secret Army*, *Return of the Saint*, *Edward VIII*, *The Professionals*, *My Son, My Son*, *Jackanory*, *Shalkin*, *The Gate of Eden*, *The Potting Shed*, *The Double Dealer*, *The Agatha Christie Hour*, *Minder*, *The Treasure Seekers*, *The Home Front*, *Chinese Detective*, *The Old Men at the Zoo*, *Martin Luther – Heretic* and *Strange Tales*. Maurice has appeared in many films including *From a Far Country* and *Julia*.

Maurice played Professor Edgeworth in 'The Twin Dilemma'. As anyone who saw the story can confirm, Maurice Denham turned in a wonderfully sensitive performance. At a party in actor Kevin McNally's flat after the final recording of 'The Twin Dilemma', Maurice agreed that he had had a marvellous time. He is a very dynamic person and still has an incredible amount of energy: he left the party at 4.30 am.

Maurice has to live on a strict diet; his favourite dish is steak and kidney pie, but because of his eating restrictions he has chosen a very simple dish for you to try.

Author's Note:
A simple but effective dish. It is also delicious served cold with home-made mayonnaise and a green salad.

Grilled Breasts of Chicken à l'Azmael

Ingredients:

4 breasts of chicken
Raw tomatoes
Black pepper

Method:
Cover the chicken breasts with a layer of raw tomatoes and sprinkle with black pepper. Place the breasts on a wire mesh and place under a medium grill. Grill slowly to make sure that the chicken cooks right through. When cooked serve with a vegetable of your choice.

Paul Conrad

Romulus Apricot Chicken

Serves 4 people

Ingredients:

4 breasts of chicken
½ medium onion (skinned and chopped)
4 rashers (slices) of bacon (chopped)
1 oz/28 g dried apricots (chopped)
3 oz/85 g rice
1 beaten egg
Tarragon
Salt and pepper to taste

Method:
Stuffing:
Fry the bacon and the onion until the onion is soft and not too brown. Add to the rice which has previously been cooked. Then add the chopped apricots. Beat in the egg and add the tarragon to taste and the salt and pepper.

Chicken:
Cut each breast into 3 portions and add the apricot stuffing. Roll back the chicken portions filled with the stuffing and secure with a cocktail stick. Place stuffed chicken in a dish. Add a knob of butter and cover the dish with tin (aluminium) foil then bake in the oven at 400°F, 200°C (Gas Mark 6) for 30–40 minutes. Drain the juice from the chicken portions and add to the sauce.

Sauce:
Ingredients:

2 oz flour (plain)
¼ pint (5 oz US) dry white wine (naughty boy)
¼ pint of double cream (large carton)
Salt and pepper.

Method:
Add the flour to juice of the chicken and cook for about 1 minute stirring continuously. Beat in the cream and wine. When completely mixed pour over the chicken.

Serve with jacket potatoes and salad of your choice. Or serve with sauté potatoes and vegetables.

Author's Note:
This dish is much more complicated than Remus Pie, but well worth the effort. I would serve a well chilled bottle of white Australian wine with this meal.

Dick Mills

Audio Effects

Dick Mills was born in Gillingham, Kent in 1936 and was educated at Sir Joseph Wiliamson's Mathematical School in Rochester. Following his National Service in the Royal Air Force (during which time, the prospect of returning to an Insurance Company in the City spurred him on to find another job), he joined the BBC as a Recording Engineer in 1956.

Two years later, and six months after the creation of the BBC Radiophonic Workshop, Dick found himself at Maida Vale on a 'helping-hand' basis. Having proved his mettle with such classics as

Quatermass and the Pit and *Major Bloodnok's Stomach* he was ready for the challenge of *Doctor Who*, assisting in the making of the signature tune with Delia Derbyshire, and in the creation and development of the TARDIS dematerialisation sound and the Dalek voice treatment with Brian Hodgson. Soon after *Doctor Who* got under way, creative partnerships broke up at the Workshop and Brian carried on solo with *Doctor Who* until he left the BBC in 1972. At this point in the Doctor's travels Dick re-entered the time-zone, completing the 'Carnival of Monsters' adventure and starting his first full *Who* story, 'The Three Doctors'.

Since then he has been responsible for the series' 'Special Sound' (actually, he's made more than one, despite friendly rumours to the contrary) and, if he can find his tin of Swarfega, he is confidently looking forward to the new season. In case you're wondering what he does for relaxation, Dick keeps tropical fish and also manages to find time to write books about them.

Krotonised Khoncie

This is the staple diet of the poorer people of Kroton. Its attraction lies in the fact that all the ingredients are available naturally, especially during the long foggy seasons when the multi-legged khoncie is captured easily. One khoncie will feed an entire village, who may take up to a whole week removing its tough armour-plated skin to get at the succulent meat beneath.

Author's Note:
A lovely amusing recipe. I hope you have fun working it out.

Ingredients:

1½ small pieces of cooked khoncie
1 large niono (sliced)
2 fresh green lhliiecs (chopped)
1 tsp/1¼ tsp/7.5 g lhliic powder
1 piece fresh toro-grenig
2 level tsps/2½ tsps/15 g crushed rankiocre seeds
1 tsp/1¼ tsp/7.5 g crushed ncimu seeds
1 level tb/1¼ tb/30 g mecritur powder
2 momacrud pods (crushed)
¼ pt/5 oz/1½ dl natural ghoutry
2 fl oz/¼ cup/50 ml khoncie stock (bouillon)
2 crushed cloves of cragli
Gonnoturd oil, tlas and wraet

Method:
Fry the niono for about 5 minutes, before adding all the spices and gragli: continue to cook for a further 5 minutes to draw out the flavours. Add khoncie pieces to the pan. Gradually stir in ghoutry and wraet, and add some tlas. Transfer to casserole and cook on a low heat for 10–15 minutes.

Serving:
The spicy dish of khoncie is best served with lipau crie anniid reclips and chango mutney, although it is seen by some as challenging fate the flavours without any such gastronomic safety-nets.

Kroton–English Dictionary (nearest equivalents)
Khoncie = Chicken
Niono = Onion
Lhliiecs = Chillies
Lhliic = Chilli
Toro-grenig = Root-ginger
Randiocre = Coriander
Ncimu = Cumin
Mecritur = Turmeric
Momacrud = Cardomum
Ghoutry = Yoghurt
Cragli = Garlic
Gonnoturd = Groundnut
Lipau Crie = Pilau rice
Anniid keclips = Indian pickles
Chango mutney = Mango Chutney
Tlas = Salt
Wraet = Water

Beryl Reid

Briggs in 'Earthshock'

Beryl Reid was born on June 17, 1920 in Hereford, England. She was educated at Ladyborn House, Withington High, and Levenshulme High. She made her first stage appearance in *Concert Party* in Bridlington in 1936 but really made her name with the British audiences when she created a character called Monica, in *Educating Archie* on radio.

She has performed on TV, radio, clubs, variety shows and revues, including the famous Half Past Eight Shows in Edinburgh, in which she appeared in 427 sketches in one season. Beryl's first serious stage-play was *The Killing of Sister George* in 1965 in the West End of London. She followed this with *Entertaining Mr Sloane* some years later, and appeared in the film version of both plays. Her other stage credits include *Blythe Spirit*, *Romeo and Juliet*, *Spring Awakening*, *Campiello* for the National Theatre, and *The Way of the World* at the Royal Shakespeare Company.

Beryl has largely concentrated on TV in recent years including *The Rivals*, *Dear Father*, *The Harry Secombe Show*, *The Goodies*, and the English Old Time Music Hall show, *The Good Old Days*. Her most dramatic and, in my opinion, her best performance was in *Tinker, Tailor, Soldier, Spy* and its sequel *Smiley's People* on which I also worked. Her films have included *The Belles of St Trinians*, *Star*, *Inspector Clouseau*, *The Beast in the Cellar*, *No Sex Please We're British*, and *The Dock Brief*.

Beryl has been married twice and her hobbies include gardening, cooking and driving.

Briggs' Poulet à l'Orange

Serves 4 people

Ingredients:

1 tsp/1 ¼ tsp/7.5 g mixed herbs
4 chicken joints
Juice of 6 oranges (or ¾ tin of unsweetened orange juice)
1 tsp/1 ¼ tsp/7.5 g ground cinnamon
1 tsp/1 ¼ tsp/7.5 g ground ginger
1 tsp/1 ¼ tsp/7.5 g ground nutmeg
1 tsp/1 ¼ tsp/7.5 g ground mixed spice
1 dessertspoon plain flour
Butter or margarine
Salt and pepper

Method:

Mix all the cinnamon, ginger, nutmeg, mixed spice and flour, until they make a pale brown powder.

Fry the chicken joints in butter or margarine with one teaspoonful of mixed herbs. Remove from the heat and frying pan, add more fat to the pan and blend in the pale brown powder to make a roux. Slowly add the juices of six oranges or ¾ of a tin of unsweetened orange juice to make a thick sauce. Put the pieces of chicken in a casserole dish and add the orange gravy with salt and pepper to taste and cook for about 90 minutes on 350°F, 180°C (Gas Mark 4) until the chicken is tender. Serve with rice and a salad.

Author's Note:

The sauce brings a new dimension to the chicken, giving an old favourite an exciting taste.

Michael Gough

The Celestial Toymaker in 'The Celestial Toymaker' and Hedin in 'Arc of Infinity'

Michael Gough was born in Malaya in 1917 and has been one of our leading actors in the theatre, TV and films for many years. He first appeared in *Doctor Who* in 'The Celestial Toymaker', and was married to Anneke Wills, who played the role of Polly, one of the Doctor's companions.

He has many TV series to his credit including *Vincent the Dutchman*, *Shoulder to Shoulder*, *Fall of Eagles*, *George Sand* and *Shades of Green*. His films include *Women in Love*, *Velvet House*, *Julius Caesar*, *Trog*, *The Go-Between*, *Henry VIII and his Six Wives*, *Horror Hospital*, and most recently *The Boys from Brazil* and *Memed, My Hawk*.

Celestial Chicken or Paradisical Peacock

Ingredients:

1 lb/453 g chicken breasts or peacock breasts
½ tsp/¾ tsp/3 g salt
1 egg white (keep the yolk for later)
1 tb/1¼ tb cornflour (cornstarch)
1 sweet red pepper
2 tbs/2½ tbs/38 ml oil
2 tbs/2½ tbs/60 g lard
2 dried chilli peppers
1 tb/1¼ tb/30 g chopped onion
1 slice of root ginger (chopped)
1 tb/1¼ tb/19 ml soya sauce
1 tb/1¼ tb/19 ml dry sherry
2 tsps/2½ tsps/12.5 ml tomato purée (paste)
1 tsp/1¼ tsp/6.2 ml wine vinegar
1 tb/1¼ tb/19 ml chicken broth

Method:

Dice the chicken or peacock into small cubes and rub salt into it. Beat the egg white for 5 seconds and add cornflour to make a batter. Mix the cubed chicken or peacock evenly with the batter. Slice sweet pepper into smallish pieces. Heat 2 tablespoons of oil in a frying pan over a moderate heat. Add chicken or peacock all spread out. Stir-fry for two minutes and remove. Add lard to the pan and then the chilli peppers, onion, ginger, and sweet red pepper. Stir-fry for 1½ minutes. Add the soya sauce, sherry, tomato purée, wine vinegar and chicken broth, and stir fry together for 30 seconds. Return the chicken or peacock to the pan and stir-fry together for another 30 seconds. Turn out on a dish and serve.

Author's Note:

Michael Gough has suggested that this dish might be accompanied by ice-cold lager, perhaps because of the chilli peppers. Celestial Chicken could be served on a bed of rice.

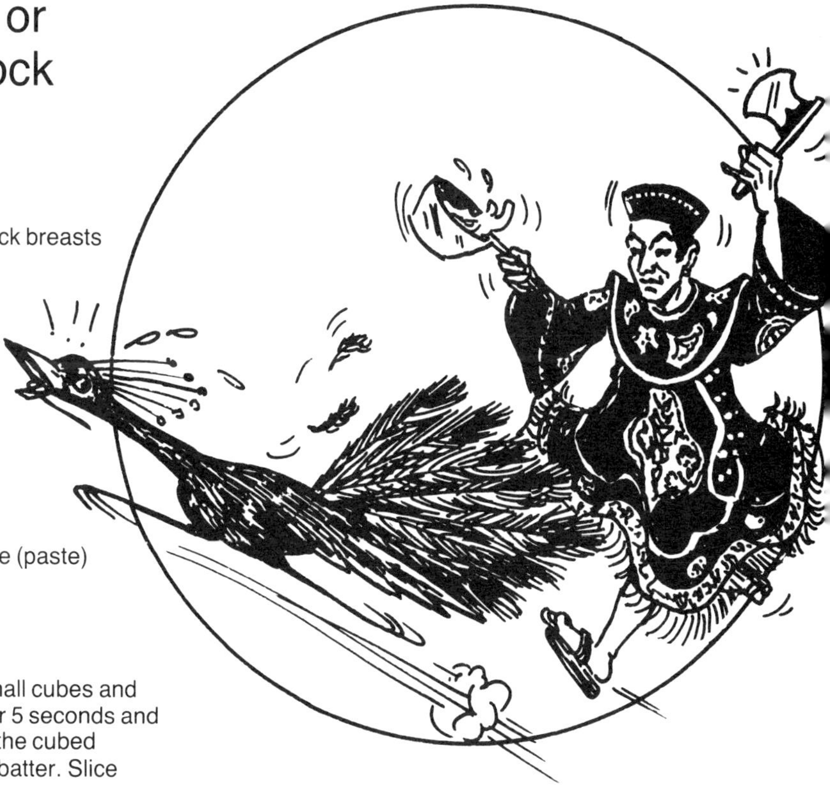

Dave Chapman

Video Effects

Dave was born on July 17, 1951, in Formby, Lancashire. He was educated at Waterloo Grammar School, and Seaforth College Liverpool, during which time he provided the lighting for school plays, amateur dramatic groups and discos. He left school at eighteen and worked for six months at Ironbridge Power Station.

Dave joined the BBC in January 1970, and began work on video effects in 1974. His first big show was *The Chester Mystery Plays*.

Dave's favourite productions include *Jane* and its sequel *Jane in the Desert* and, of course, *Doctor Who*.

Chicken Boogaloo

Serves 4 people

Ingredients:

Flesh from 4 chicken joints
2 oz/56 g flour
2 oz/56 g butter
2 large chopped onions
1 large peeled apple (or ripe mango)
3 cloves garlic
3 tsps/3¾ tsps/22 g garam marsala powder
1 tb/1¼ tb/30 g paprika
1 tb/1¼ tb/30 g mango chutney
2 bay leaves
1 tsp/1¼ tsp/6.2 ml Worcester sauce
½ tsp/3 g ground or fresh ginger
½ tsp/3 g cinnamon
¼ pt/5 oz/1½ dl plain yoghurt
¾ pt/15 oz/4.5 dl light stock (bouillon)
Sultanas
Chopped red and/or green pepper

Method:

Put the flour, apple, garlic, paprika, chutney, Worcester sauce, ginger, cinnamon, yoghurt and stock in liquidizer and blend. Fry the onions in butter until soft. Add the chicken meat and fry for 5 minutes. Add contents of liquidizer and sultanas and bring to the boil, stirring constantly. Gently simmer for 45 minutes, stirring occasionally. Add chopped pepper and cook for a further 15 minutes. Remove bay leaves. Add garam masala powder. Stir thoroughly. Serve with rice, green salad, chutneys etc.

Author's Note:

A very eastern flavour, and one that I like very much. This recipe brings a new flavour and dimension to traditional chicken. Really scrumptious!

Dinah Sheridan

Chancellor Flavia in 'The Five Doctors'

Dinah Sheridan appeared in her first play, *Where the Rainbow Ends*, at the age of twelve, and in her first film when she was sixteen. Her films include *The Story of Shirley Yorke*, *The Gilbert and Sullivan Story*, *Sound Barrier*, *Appointment in London*, *Where No Vultures Fly* and *The Railway Children*, but inevitably she will be best remembered for *Genevieve*. In 1954 she gave up acting to bring up her two children (one of whom, Jenny Hanley, has made quite a name for herself in her own right) and returned in 1967 to star in *Let's All Go Down the Strand* at the Phoenix Theatre. This was followed by *A Boston Story* at the Duchess and *Out of the Question* at the St Martin's. She also stared in *Move Over Mrs Markham* at the Vaudeville Theatre, *The Card*, at the Queen's Theatre, *The Gentle Hook* at the Piccadilly, and co-starred with Douglas Fairbanks Junior in *The Pleasure of his Company* at the Phoenix. She also played in a *A Murder is Announced* at the Vaudeville and she went to Brighton and Canada with Sir John Geilgud in *Half Life*.

Dinah has made many television appearances, the latest being *The Swish of the Curtain* for the BBC and a pilot for *Just Liz* for Thames. Most recently she made guest appearances in the films *The Mirror Cracked* and *House of Hammer* and has just completed a BBC Radio play, *Rainer Maria Rilke*, and *The Lady of Duino*.

Dinah's most recent stage appearance was in the long West End run of *Present Laughter* with Donald Sinden, and on TV she has been seen in two series of *Don't Wait Up* and has starred in Yorkshire TV's recent success, *Winning Streak*.

Chancellor Flavia's Chicken Favourite

Ingredients:

4 boned chicken breasts
1 tsp/1¼ tsp/7.5 g dried tarragon
Finely grated rind of 1 lemon
1 clove of garlic, peeled and crushed
2 oz/56 g butter
4 tbs/5 tbs/120 g dried breadcrumbs
Salt and pepper

Method:

Pre-heat the oven to 375°F, 190°C (Gas Mark 5).

Lay the chicken breasts flat and make a deep slit in the side of the plumpest part, making sure not to cut the chicken completely in half.

Put the tarragon, lemon rind, garlic and butter in a small bowl, season with the salt and pepper and mix well with a knife, then gently stuff the mixture evenly into the slit of each chicken breast. Close the slits with cocktail sticks and brush the breasts with a little oil.

Coat each breast in breadcrumbs, place on a oiled baking tray and cook for 45 minutes. Finally garnish with wedges of lemon and sprigs of parsley. This dish is good with very new potatoes, or baked potatoes in their jackets.

Author's Note:

I have had this dish many times and it is one of my favourites. If you are on a diet I suggest that you remove the skin first before preparing the chicken as that is the fattiest part of the bird. A lovely mixed salad would be good instead of potatoes or vegetables. Serve a lovely chilled dry white wine during the meal.

VEGETARIAN DISHES

Jacqueline Hill

Barbara Wright – companion to the first Doctor

Jacqueline Hill played the part of Barbara Wright for the first two seasons of *Doctor Who*. Her first show was 'An Unearthly Child', and her final appearance was in 'The Chase', making a total of sixteen stories. She started training as an actress at RADA and went on to make a name for herself on British as well as American TV.

Jacqueline retired in the late 1960s to get married and raise a family. She and her husband, the well known TV director Alan Rakoff, have two children. She returned to acting in the late 1970s to appear in a stage play, and then appeared in a BBC TV production of *Romeo and Juliet*, which was directed by her husband. She has also appeared in the very popular ITV series *Tales of the Unexpected*. She returned to *Doctor Who* briefly in 1980 as Lexa in 'Meglos'.

Here then is Jacqueline's very pleasant and versatile dish. This could be a first course, a pâté, or a dip. I am sure you will get a lot of pleasure deciding for yourself.

Aubergine Mac

Ingredients:

2 large aubergines (eggplants)
1 chopped medium onion
Juice of 1 lemon
1 chopped green pepper
1 clove of garlic
¼–½ pt/5–10 oz/⅛–¼ litre sunflower or olive oil
Salt and pepper, to taste
Large handful of parsley

Method:
Bake the aubergines in a medium oven (350°F, 180°C, Gas Mark 4) until the aubergines are soft. Remove them from the oven and let them cool. When they are cool, open the aubergines and remove the flesh. Put the flesh into a liquidiser, then add the chopped onion, the chopped green pepper and the juice of the lemon, the parsley and finally the garlic. Whisk or blend furiously until it becomes a smooth paste. Then add the salt and pepper to taste and whisk again. Now with the machine turned on slowly start to pour the oil through the funnel (as in making mayonnaise) until the mixture is the correct medium consistency. Cover and put the mixture into a fridge for at least 8 hours.

Serving Suggestions:
1) On hot toast with drinks.
2) As a dip.
3) Place onto lettuce and decorate with tomatoes.

Author's Note:
The fact that this dish can be served in three different ways I find very attractive.

Peter Moffatt

Viennese Cabbage

Ingredients:

1 red cabbage
2 tbs/2½ tbs/60 g sugar
2 tbs/2½ tbs/60 g butter
3 tbs/3¾ tbs/57 ml wine vinegar
1 dessertspoon flour
2 tbs/2½ tbs/38 ml water

Method:
Chop up the cabbage into small pieces. (Don't shred it as it is inclined to go a bit gooey if you do.) Remove the hard centre stalk. In a large saucepan put 2 tablespoons of butter. Add the 2 tablespoons of sugar, and let it cook, stirring now and then until it goes a light brown. Add the chopped-up cabbage and toss until it is thoroughly coated with the sugar. Reduce the heat and keep stirring for 2 or 3 minutes. Then add 2 tablespoons of water and three tablespoons of wine vinegar.

In a frying pan heat 1 dessertspoon of butter and gradually stir in 1 dessertspoon of flour. When this has browned, add a little of the liquid from the cabbage saucepan to it. Cook gently, stirring occasionally for 10 minutes then serve.

Author's Note:
This is a colourful dish as well as tasty and goes well with soya meat stew, accompanied by fresh garden peas. It also goes well with Moffatta's Moussaka.

Jacqueline Pearce

Chessene in 'The Two Doctors'

Jacqueline was educated in a Convent and being an impressionable child she wished to take the veil. Alas, parental opposition deemed this impossible, so she decided to become an actress instead. She left the convent and won a scholarship to the Royal Academy of Dramatic Art. She also studied at the Actors' Studio in America for three years. She made her acting debut in the Hammer Horror movies, *The Plague of the Zombies*, and *The Reptile*, where she played the girl who turned into a poisonous reptile, and she also co-starred with Jerry Lewis in *Don't Raise the Bridge, Lower the River*. Her favourite role in the West End has been in *Otherwise Engaged*, directed by Harold Pinter, and among her TV credits are *The Philanthropist*, *Measure for Measure*, *Blake's Seven* (in which she played Servalan), and *Doctor Who*.

She would like to be remembered for her erotic poetry but has yet to find a publisher of sufficient gall. Jacqueline loves travelling and is passionate about food, wine, and astrology. She adores her work and Joel, with whom she lives on a boat in Chelsea.

Casserole à la Chessene

Ingredients:

1 lb/453 g chopped onions
3 cloves of crushed garlic
1 lb/453 g chopped mushrooms
1 lb/453 g chopped courgettes
1 large tin of tomatoes
1 glass of red wine (optional)
1 tb/1 ¼ tb/30 g mixed herbs
½ lb/200 g Gruyère cheese

Method:
Fry the onions, garlic, mushrooms and courgettes until soft. Then in a large casserole dish, place the fried ingredients with a large tin of tomatoes, add the red wine and 1 tablespoon of mixed herbs. Then sprinkle the Gruyère cheese on the top and bake in the oven (356°F, 180°C, Gas Mark 4) for 45 minutes.

Author's Note:
This dish is also delicious when served cold. Alternatively it can be used to accompany some of the main course recipes in this book.

Barry Letts

Producer of Doctor Who *1969–1974*

Barry joined the BBC Director's Course in 1966, having previously been an actor and a writer. After directing *The Newcomers*, *Z-Cars* and two children's serials, he became, in 1969, the producer of *Doctor Who*. He continued in this job until 1974, after casting Tom Baker as the replacement for Jon Pertwee. During this period he also directed a number of *Doctor Who* stories.

In 1975, he became Producer of the BBC-1 Classic Serial (which is transmitted at Sunday teatime) and has held this position ever since. His recent productions have included *A Tale of Two Cities* which won an Emmy award, *Great Expectations* and *Jane Eyre*, both of which were nominated for BAFTA awards, *Beau Geste*, *Goodbye Mr Chips*, *The Mill on the Floss*, *Sense and Sensibility*, *Dombey and Son*, *The Old Curiosity Shop*, and *Gulliver in Lilliput*, which he dramatised and directed.

Having worked with Barry on *Treasure Island* as an Assistant Floor Manager, we have remained friends ever since. Barry has devised a rather amusing story to accompany his recipe and I hope you enjoy it.

?

(This recipe is unnamed, but having read the story with it I am sure the reader will come up with some ideas.)

I first tasted this dish during a ghastly location shoot on Venus in 1972 (I think). Terrible, I do know. The rain, being sulphuric acid, kept rotting large holes in the BBC umbrellas. We were plagued by dragonflies (and a Venusian dragonfly breathing real fire) and the Furgle-handlers went on strike.

I think we would have all joined them if it hadn't been for the location caterers. Even on Earth, location caterers have three hands. How else could they produce two hundred meals from a tiny van in an hour or so's work? On Venus they have six hands each; the results are out of this world (to coin a phrase). Yet the most delicious Venusian dish of all is also the cheapest, easiest and quickest. Here it is.

Ingredients:

3 oz/85 g per head of blim tree worms
4 oz/113 g per head of runcle grease
1 oz/28 g per head of nossy bulbs
Grated snadge, to taste

Method:

Boil the worms *al dente* (15–20 minutes). Crush the nossy cloves and fry lightly in the melted runcle grease. Stir in the worms, season to taste and serve with a sprinkling of grated snadge. *Note:* Some of these ingredients may be difficult to find since the Venusian shop in Knightsbridge went bust. An equally delicious version can be produced by replacing worms with spaghetti, the runcle grease with unsalted butter; the nossy cloves with garlic and the snadge with parmesan or cheddar cheese.

Author's Note:

Well, I bet that was a surprise for you! When made with the ingredients from Earth, it is delicious, especially with Mena's Tachyonic Sauce!

I cannot comment on the Venusian version as I could not find the ingredients anywhere. However how about trying a lovely chilled bottle of Italian white to go with this? I think a very chilled bottle of Frascati Gotto d'Oro 1982 – the wine that the Romans drink.

Elisabeth Sladen

Sarah Jane Smith – Companion to the third and fourth Doctors

Elisabeth Sladen joined *Doctor Who* in 1973 in 'The Time Warrior' with Jon Pertwee. She then went on to appear with Jon in 'Invasion of the Dinosaurs', 'Death to the Daleks', 'The Monster of Peladon', 'Planet of the Spiders', and with Tom Baker in 'Robot', 'The Ark in Space', 'The Sontaran Experiment', 'Genesis of the Daleks', 'Revenge of the Cybermen', 'Terror of the Zygons', 'Planet of Evil', 'Pyramids of Mars', 'The Android Invasion', 'The Brain of Morbius', 'The Seeds of Doom', 'The Masque of Mandragora', and 'The Hand of Fear', in which she left the series.

Since leaving *Doctor Who* Lis has never stopped working. She appeared in the Children's Classic *Gulliver in Lilliput* for BBC TV. She also spent a season at the Bristol Old Vic where she appeared in *Twelfth Night*.

Lis recreated her role as Sarah Jane starring in *K9 and Company* which was enormously successful. She also appeared in 'The Five Doctors', for the twentieth anniversary of *Doctor Who*. Lis is also a regular visitor to the United States appearing at *Doctor Who* Conventions. She is married to actor, Brian Miller, who occasionally accompanies her at conventions. Lis had promised an old favourite recipe, but I am sure it will be just as popular as Sarah Jane.

Cauliflower Cheese

Serves 4 hungry people

Ingredients:

1 large cauliflower
½ lb/226 g roughly chopped onions
2 oz/56 g black olives (unstoned if possible)
2 cloves of garlic
½ can of anchovy fillets (optional)
8 tbs/10 tbs/172 ml olive oil
7 fl oz/1 cup/¼ litre red wine
1 oz/28 g Parmesan cheese
1 oz/28 g grated farmhouse cheddar cheese, mixed with the Parmesan
Few sprigs of parsley

Method:

Trim the outer leaves of the cauliflower and cut away the tough stalk end. Chop the onions roughly. Use a flame-proof casserole or a heavy based pan into which the whole cauliflower will fit snugly. First pour the oil into the pan or dish and warm it. Add the onions and cook them gently for about 10 minutes, until softened.

Meanwhile, cut up the olives and put into a bowl. Crush the garlic and add to the olives and then stir in the wine. Lift the anchovy fillets out of the can (keeping the oil) and add them to the casserole, crushing them gently with the back of a wooden spoon. They will disintegrate quite quickly. Blend them into the warm oil.

Tip the contents of the bowl into the casserole and bring to the boil, stirring. Lay the whole cauliflower in the casserole, stalk-end down. Pour the anchovy oil over the cauliflower and sprinkle with the mixed grated cheese. Cover the casserole dish with a lid and cook over very low heat until the cauliflower is tender. The base is cooked in the liquid, and the florets will cook in the steam.

Lift the cooked cauliflower out of the casserole on to a hot serving dish and keep it warm in a low oven for a few minutes while you boil the sauce, to reduce it a little and concentrate its flavour. Check the sauce for seasoning (although this is not normally needed). Pour it over the cauliflower and sprinkle the coarsely chopped parsley on top. Serve straight away with fresh baked bread and wine.

Author's Note:
Adding the wine to the sauce brings a whole new dimension to this traditional dish of cauliflower cheese.

Jon Pertwee

Poached Egg Salad

Serves 6 people

Ingredients:

6 eggs
6 slices of peeled tomatoes
Lettuce leaves for garnish
Salt and pepper, to taste
8 fl oz/1 cup/¼ litre mayonnaise
2 fl oz/¼ cup/50 ml chilli sauce or ½ tsp/¾ tsp/3 g chilli powder
½ tsp/¾ tsp/3 g chopped basil
2 tsps/2½ tsps/15 g chopped chives
2 tsps/2½ tsps/15 g chopped parsley

Method:
Poach the eggs and lift out carefully and place in cold water. The eggs will have to be trimmed when placed on the main dish. Arrange each tomato slice on a bed of lettuce, and sprinkle the tomatoes with salt and pepper. Then sprinkle a little of the chopped basil and put on top one of the well-drained eggs that has been trimmed. Mix the mayonnaise with the chilli sauce (or powder), and also with the ½ teaspoon of basil, chives and parsley. Pour this over the eggs. Place in the fridge to chill before serving.

Author's Note:
Simple and very tasty. The overall preparation time is 30 minutes.

Matthew Waterhouse

Adric – Companion to the fourth and fifth Doctors

Matthew Waterhouse was born on December 19, 1961 in Hertford. He later moved to Sussex with his parents. He was educated at St Wilfrid's Primary School (Haywards Heath) and then at Shoreham (Independent) Grammar School. After gaining seven 'O' Levels and three 'A' Levels he left school and took temporary jobs in a warehouse and a kitchen. He worked for the BBC at Lime Grove cutting up newspapers for the News Information Department.

His previous television experience was in the very successful BBC TV Series *To Serve Them All My Days* (Episodes one and two). His hobbies include movies, expensive books, science fiction and horror.

Matthew joined *Doctor Who* as Adric in 'Full Circle' and appeared in 'State of Decay', 'Warriors' Gate', 'The Keeper of Traken', 'Logopolis', 'Castrovalva', 'Four to Doomsday', 'Kinda', 'The Visitation', 'Black Orchid', and finally 'Earthshock', where Adric met his doom and was blown to pieces.

Matthew was very amusing when I had to teach him a few dance steps for 'Black Orchid'. He was very clever and suggested to the director that Adric only had to do about three steps before he made a bee-line for the buffet table in order to spend the entire musical interlude eating. I tease him about it every time I see him.

Mushroom Pancakes in Hollandaise Sauce

Serves 2 people

The Batter: Ingredients:

4 oz/100 g plain wholemeal flour
½ pt/10 oz/3 dl milk
1 egg
Sea salt

Method:

Sieve together the flour and a small pinch of sea salt. Add the egg, and stir briefly. Pour in the milk and stir thoroughly. Beat well. The mix should become smooth and creamy. Put in the fridge for at least 30 minutes. Remember to beat again before using the batter.

The Filling: Ingredients:

8 oz/225 g fresh mushrooms
1 tb/1 ¼ tb/19 ml oil

Method:

Heat the oil and lightly fry the mushrooms, having first washed, peeled and sliced them. Then drain the mushrooms in a paper towel. Cover and keep warm.

The Sauce: Ingredients:

2 oz/50 g polyunsaturated margarine
1 oz/25 g plain wholemeal flour
½ pt/10 oz/3 dl milk
1 small egg yolk
Squeeze of lemon juice
Parsley
Salt and pepper, to taste

Method:

Melt the 1 oz of margarine in a pan. Add the flour, then cook, then add the milk. Stir thoroughly as you bring the mix to the boil. When thickened, remove it from the heat and leave to cool for a few minutes. Beat the rest of the ingredients into the sauce with the salt and pepper to taste.

Finally fill the pancakes with the mushrooms and fold them over. Pour on the sauce and sprinkle with chopped parsley.

Louise Jameson

Leela – Companion to the fourth Doctor

Louise Jameson joined *Doctor Who* in 1977 as the savage Leela and stayed with the series until 1978. Her first appearance as Leela was in 'The Face of Evil' and she then appeared in 'The Robots of Death', 'The Talons of Weng-Chiang', 'Horror of Fang Rock', 'The Invisible Enemy', 'Image of The Fendahl', 'The Sun Makers', 'Underworld' (on which I also worked) and 'The Invasion of Time'. She was one of the most popular companions of all time and was a great favourite with the male viewers for obvious reasons.

When I worked with Louise on 'Underworld', we had a terrific time. In fact, Louise is just the opposite to Leela. She is very gentle, kind and considerate, and she hates violence. After she left *Doctor Who* she went to Bristol to join the Bristol Old Vic company.

Louise was trained at the famous drama school RADA, and since she left in 1970 has been a very successful actress. Since 1981 she has been appearing in the well known series called *Tenko*, playing a cockney woman called Blanche imprisoned by the Japanese during the second world war.

Louise was born on April 20, 1951 in London's East End. She has a lovely little son called Harry and Louise is devoted to him.

Leela's Savage Savoury

Ingredients:

1 large chopped onion
1 pinch chilli powder
1 pinch ginger
1 tsp/1 1/4 tsp/7.5 g nutmeg
2 small courgettes (zucchini)
1 small finely chopped green pepper
1 small finely chopped red cabbage
Black pepper and salt, to taste
Olive oil
1 small carton single (light) cream

Method:

Fry the chopped onion in olive oil until soft but not brown, then add the black pepper, salt, a touch of chilli powder, a touch of ginger and a teaspoon of nutmeg. Mix this and fry with the onions. Then add the two chopped courgettes the chopped green pepper and red cabbage and continue to cook. If it starts drying out, add a little water. Simmer for 10–15 minutes. Then add a small carton of single cream and mix in well with the rest of the sauce.

Author's Note:

This is delicious and simple to make. Louise tells me this may be served with rice and kidney beans. A nutritious dish for vegetarians.

DESSERTS

Fiona Cumming

Planet of Fire Pudding

Ingredients:

3 egg whites
6 oz/171 g caster sugar
Pinch of cream of tartar
3 oz/85 g nibbed almond
½ pt/10 oz/3 dl double (heavy) cream
Vanilla essence
Fruit (raspberries or strawberries)

Method:
Separate the eggs. (Keep the yolks for lemon curd, thickening a sauce, having scrambled egg, or making a face mask). Whip the whites till they become very stiff. Start putting sugar in at 2 tablespoons at a time, and whip for a full minute before putting in the next 2 tablespoons of sugar. When half the sugar is left, this may be folded in with the cream of tartar, and the almonds. Take care not to break the bubbles in the egg white.

Cover two flat trays with foil and cover the foil with oil and flour. Place the mixture on the trays, pushing it into two circles roughly 8 inches or 9 inches in diameter. Cook for an hour in a low oven (350°F, 180°C, Gas Mark 4). If they are ready they will lift off the foil, if not put them back to dry out for another 15 minutes. Cool on a wire tray. This can be done the day before they are needed. Whip the cream with a little caster sugar and the vanilla flavouring. Place one meringue upside down on a serving plate and put half of the cream on the flat base, cover the cream with fruit and top this with the second meringue and decorate with the remaining cream and serve with whole fruit.

Author's Note:
Meringue is one of my favourite desserts. By adding fruit you get the experience of the sweetness of the cream and meringue with the flavour of the fruit.

Maureen O'Brien

Rhubarb Chumbly

Serves 4–6 people

Ingredients:
Topping:

3 oz/75 g butter or margarine
6 oz/150 g flour (plain)
2 oz/50 g sugar (caster or demerara)
2 oz/50 g nuts (chopped, optional)
Grated rind of ½ a lemon

Filling:
1 lb/453 g rhubarb
3–4 oz/75–100 g sugar

Method:
Wash and clean the rhubarb very well then cut into 1 inch sections. Place the fruit into a greased dish (oven-proof) and add 3–4 oz (75–100 g) of sugar. Prepare the topping by rubbing the fat into the flour and adding the rest of the sugar, nuts and lemon rind. Sprinkle over the fruit and bake in an oven 428°F, 220°C (Gas Mark 7) for about 40–50 minutes. Serve hot with either custard or cream.

Author's Note:
I prefer to serve double cream or whipped cream with my rhubarb crumble and I don't include nuts. You can also make this dish using any combination of fruits that you might like.

Heather Hartnell

Special Chocolate Chumblies

Ingredients:

6 oz/171 g butter or margarine
6 oz/171 g caster sugar
5 oz/143 g self-raising flour
2 oz/56 g sifted cocoa

For the Coffee Cream:
4 oz/113 g butter
Sifted icing sugar
1 dessertspoon instant coffee
1 dessertspoon brandy or medium sherry

For the Topping
¼ lb/113 g dark chocolate

Method:
Blend the butter or margarine together, then add the eggs one by one, and finally the flour and cocoa. Put the mixture into little bun tins or cases, and bake for 15 to 20 minutes at 375°F, 190°C (Gas Mark 4).

Melt the chocolate, then spread thinly onto greaseproof paper on a flat surface. When cold and set, cut into squares about 1½ inch large.

Make the coffee cream by beating the butter with as much icing sugar as it will hold. Add the coffee dissolved in a dessert-spoonful of hot water, then add the brandy or sherry.

When the buns are almost cool, top with a good splodge of cream, then cap with a chocolate square.

Author's Note:
Another favourite of William 'Bill' Hartnell, and still a Hartnell family winner!

Cyril Luckham

The White Guardian

Cyril Luckham is one of our best known character actors. He was born on July 25, 1907, in Salisbury, Wiltshire and was educated at the Royal Navy College, Osborne, and the Royal Naval College at Dartmouth. He originally wanted a career in the Royal Navy, but unfortunately he was invalided out in 1931 as a Lieutenant. He trained for the stage with The Arthur Brough Players and the Folkestone Dramatic School. His first stage appearance was as the footman in *The Admirable Crichton* at the Folkestone Theatre. Then there followed theatre appearances in Folkestone, Manchester, Bristol, Coventry, and Southport. Cyril was also a member of the Royal Shakespeare Company for three seasons.

Cyril has been in more stage plays, TV plays and series than he can remember. His West End plays include: *The Family Reunion*, *Photo Finish*, and *You Never Can Tell*. His film credits are *Anne of a Thousand Days*, *A Man for all Seasons*, *The Pumpkin Eater*, *The Naked Runners* and *Providence*. Some of his TV appearances include *The Forsyte Saga*, *Public Eye*, *Jennie*, *The Cedar Tree*, *Wodehouse Playhouse*, *What Every Woman Knows*, *The Camerons*, *The Omega Factor*, *Murder at the Wedding*, *My Son, My Son*, *North and South*, *Donkey's Years*, *To Serve Them all my Days*, *The Winter's Tale*, *Tales of the Unexpected*, *The Brack Report*, *The Potting Shed*, and *Jackanory*.

Guard's Pudding

Serves 4 people

Ingredients:

¼ lb/113 g butter
¼ lb/113 g caster sugar
1 tb/1¼ tb/19 ml raspberry jam (jelly)
2 eggs
½ lb/226 g flour
½ tsp/3 g baking powder
2–3 tbs/2½–3¾ tbs/57 ml milk

Method:

Blend together the butter and sugar until the texture becomes creamy and the sugar has been dissolved. Then stir in the jam. Beat in the eggs one by one. Then sift in the flour and baking powder and stir into the mixture. Add milk as required. Then turn into a buttered mould or pudding basin and cover the top with buttered paper. Steam for 2 hours. Serve the pudding with vanilla ice-cream or jam sauce. I use both.

Author's Note:

A delightful dessert that could be served in summer or winter.

Nicola Bryant

Peri's Pineapple Cheesecake

Serves 10–12 people

Ingredients:

6 oz/175 g crushed digestive biscuits
1 tb/1 1/4 tb/30 g grated lemon peel
9 oz/250 g crushed canned pineapple
3 tbs/3 3/4 tbs/45 ml lemon juice
3 1/2 fl oz/6 2/3 tb/1 dl double (heavy) cream
4 medium sized eggs
11 oz/300 g caster sugar
3 oz/75 g melted butter
1 lb 11oz/750 g curd cheese
1 tsp/1 1/4 tsp/7.5 g salt
1 oz/25 g flour
Pineapple to decorate (optional)

Method:

Heat the oven to 325°F, 175°C (Gas Mark 3). To make the crumb mixture melt the butter and add the biscuit crumbs. Add 1 teaspoon of lemon zest and 2 oz of sugar and mix. This is the base. Use 60 ml (4 tablespoons) of mixture to line the tin and cover the crust with the drained pineapple.

To make the filling sieve the curd cheese. Add the salt and flour, remaining lemon zest, lemon juice and thick cream. Beat well. Beat the eggs with the remaining sugar till the mixture is light and fluffy. Fold into the cheese mixture. Pour the filling into the tin and sprinkle the top with the remaining crumb mixture.

Bake the cheesecake for 1 hour. Then turn off the heat and allow the cheesecake to remain in the oven for another hour. Remove the cheesecake from the oven at the end of the second hour and place on a wire rack to cool. When completely cool remove from the tin by releasing the rim. Decorate with the extra pineapple.

Author's Note:

This is a cheesecake from my childhood that I have rediscovered thanks to Peri. I adore this recipe. Many cheesecakes are too gooey and heavy, and are usually smothered with syrupy fruit. However this cake is light and pleasant to eat and just like the cheesecake my mother used to make.

This will make a lovely dish to serve with afternoon tea, which we English love to indulge in so much.

Lynda Baron

Ephemeral Pudding

Not only does this dessert not last a second, once your guests taste it, it takes no time at all to make (and impresses the hell out of them).

Ingredients:

1 sponge cake
¼ pt/5 oz/1½ dl strong black coffee
As much brandy or rum as you want
1 pt/20 oz/6 dl whipped cream
Toasted almonds

Method:
Take any old plain sponge cake, place it in a pudding basin and pour the coffee and brandy mixture over it. Push the sponge cake gently into the basin until it takes the shape of the basin. Then leave it in the fridge to settle. When it has settled (soaked up most of the liquid) turn onto a suitable dish, and cover the by now rough volcano shape with whipped cream and toasted almonds.

Lynda says, 'Do not stint on the brandy or rum and don't tell anyone how to make it. It drives them mad.'

Author's Note:
Here is a bit of a problem: Lynda Baron says that her Ephemeral Pudding is the best, Sarah Sutton says that her Brandy Sponge Cake is the best. I have put both desserts together and leave the rest up to you. There is only a slight difference in the texture of the two desserts – the sponge fingers being slightly crunchier than the cake. I like both!

Matthew Robinson

Doctor Who's Fruit Bombs

Ingredients:

4 large pears (not too ripe)
1 lb/453 g ripe red plums (tinned plums will do)
Soft brown sugar, to taste
½ pt/10 oz/3 dl double (heavy) cream (or natural yoghurt for weight watchers)
Pinch of cinnamon
1 pt/20 oz/6 dl boiling water

Method:
Remove the stones from the plums. Quarter them and boil in water, stirring vigorously until the fruit has broken up and formed a 'mush'.

Reduce the heat but continue to boil, adding the :innamon and sugar, for a further five minutes. Top, ail and peel the pears. Place pears in a casserole lish with lid and pour plum mixture over them. Cook n a low oven for two hours. Remove the pears and allow the plum mixture to cool thoroughly. When cold, beat in the cream (or yoghurt) and continue to whisk until the mixture has reached the desired consistency. Place the pears on a serving dish and spoon over the plum-cream mixture. Chill in the fridge.

Author's Note:
This is a perfect summer dessert. The sweetness and the slight tartness of the plums give a very unusual taste. However, this dish is really for when you have time to make it, as it does take about two hours. I would make this dessert the day before and put in the fridge overnight. I think a lovely sparkling wine or even champagne would go down very well with this dessert. It must be chilled, of course!

Liza Goddard

Kari in 'Terminus'

Liza Goddard was born on January 20, 1950 in Winchester. She was educated at Farnham Girls Grammar School, and the Arts Educational Trust. She started her acting career with the Farnham Repertory Company. In 1965 she went to Australia with her family, and acted on Australian TV, her most famous role being in *Skippy*. In 1969 she decided to return to England where she has worked on stage, radio and TV ever since. Her stage credits include *Sign of the Times*, and *No Sex Please, We're British*, the longest running comedy in London. She has also appeared on radio in *The Victoria Line*. Her TV appearances include *Take Three Girls* and *Take Three Women*, *Yes Honestly*, *The Brothers*, *The Upchat Line*, *The Greatest*, *Blankety Blank*, *Pig in the Middle*, *Murder at the Wedding* and *Doctor Who*.

Liza is married to singer Alvin Stardust and has a son and a daughter. Her star sign is Aquarius and her hobbies include tapestry, horse riding, health foods and reading. Liza was formerly married to Colin Baker, the sixth Doctor.

When Liza appeared in *Doctor Who* she was absolutely stunning. Her first entrance was through the exploding door of a space ship. She appeared in 'Terminus', the story in which Nyssa left the series. Liza is always busy with TV appearances and her family. She has given a variation on the traditional Christmas Mince Pies, with her own shortcrust pastry.

Kari's Star Tarts

Ingredients:

1 lb/453 g flour
½ lb/226 g butter
½ lb/226 g lard
1 egg
Cold water
Large jar of mincemeat

Method:
Rub in the fat with the flour until the texture becomes like breadcrumbs. Then add the beaten egg, and a little cold water and mix until it becomes dough. Roll out the pastry thinly and cut with a pastry cutter (the size of fairy cakes or cup cakes) and put into the greased patty pans. Put a spoonful of mincemeat into each tart and top the pastry with a star. Use a star-shaped cutter and cook in a moderate oven for 20 minutes, or until done. This makes a lovely change from the usual mince pies.

Author's Note:
I love mince pies with a large helping of whipped cream. Children love them too.

The *Doctor Who* Appreciation Society of Great Britain

Society Co-ordinator: David Saunders

The *Doctor Who* Appreciation Society was formed in 1976 as a focal point for those interested in the show. It started out with a membership of seventy and soon grew to over 1,000. The Society is divided into various departments each run by a member of the Executive body. There are reference, art, photographic and convention departments. The society runs a newsletter in which appear various articles, news, and 'rumours' (there are always more than enough people supplying material for this last section!). In the newsletter there are various advertisements for *Doctor Who* merchandise and fanzines.

The Society puts out about half-a-dozen magazines for its members including the monthly newsletter, a quarterly newsletter called *TARDIS* and a twice yearly letter called *Cosmic Masque* which features stories about the Doctors and their companions.

There are also a number of events organised by the Society's convention department. There is the annual two day convention known as 'PanoptiCon' where awards are presented to various directors, writers etc. for winning stories voted by the fans during the year. The Society is co-ordinated by David Saunders who puts a large amount of energy and drive into the running of the Society. He is in his thirties, and I have found David very charming and helpful. He is the driving force behind the Society and on many occasions I have seen the hard work that David and his fellow committee members have put into running their conventions. I wish them luck for the future! David Saunders has given a great pudding which I am sure everyone will enjoy.

Rum Pudding

Serves 4 people

Ingredients:

2 tsps/2½ tsps/12.4 ml gelatine
2 tbs/2½ tbs/38 ml water
4 eggs (separated)
3 oz/85 g caster sugar
Juice and grated rind of 1 lemon
3 tbs/3¾ tbs/57 ml sweet white wine
3 tbs/3¾ tbs/57 ml rum
4 small macaroons
Stewed fruit (pineapple, peach, cherry)

Method:

Sprinkle the gelatine over the water and leave it until it becomes spongy. Place a bowl in a pan of simmering water and heat the gelatine and water until the gelatine completely dissolves. Over another pan of simmering water whisk the egg yolks, sugar, lemon rind and juice in a heatproof bowl. Whisk this mixture until it is thick and pale and then remove from the heat.

Strain the dissolved gelatine into the egg yolk mixture and stir well; add the wine and rum and fold in the egg whites which should be stiffly whisked. Spoon into the four glass dishes and chill until the mixture is set. Decorate with the pieces of fruit and the macaroons and serve.

The Conrad Twins

Twin Surprise

Serves 4 people

Ingredients:

2 pears (fresh or tinned)
6 oz/171 g soft light brown sugar (demerara)
1 oz/28 g butter
2 tbs/2½ tbs/38 ml golden syrup
4 scoops of vanilla ice cream
Walnuts
1 large carton of double (heavy) cream

Method:
Place a pan on a moderate heat and melt the butter, then add the brown sugar, the golden syrup, and the single cream. Keep stirring all the time until the mixture begins to boil. Place the pear halves in individual dishes with the centre facing upwards. Put a scoop of ice cream in the centre of the pear and pour over the Butterscotch Sauce while it is hot. Serve straight away. You can top the whole lot with a walnut and double cream if desired.

Author's Note:
This is a very simple and economical dessert to make. The surprise comes when you bite into the hot sauce and encounter the cold ice cream.

Laurence Payne

Johnny Ringo in 'The Gun Fighters'; Morix in 'The Leisure Hive'; Dastari in 'The Two Doctors'

This Old Vic-trained Shakespearean actor first appeared in *Doctor Who* way back in the sixties playing Johnny Ringo during the TARDIS's visit to the American West when Bill Hartnell's Doctor brought her to earth in the midst of the Gun Fight at the OK Corral.

Since then there have been two further appearances: first with Tom Baker's Doctor, playing Morix in 'The Leisure Hive', and then in 1985 as Dastari in 'The Two Doctors' with Patrick Troughton and Colin Baker as the second and sixth Doctors.

Laurence, now a full-time crime writer, rarely acts these days and has nine published novels on his bookshelf to prove it!

Apricots à la Dastari

Serves 3 or 4 people

Ingredients:

15 oz/429 g (large tin) apricots
2 eggs
4 oz/113 g caster sugar
4 oz/113 g butter
4 oz/113 g ground almonds
½ oz/14 g almond essence

Method:
Empty the apricots into an ovenproof dish. Cream the butter and sugar in mixing bowl and add the almond essence. Add the beaten eggs and fold in the ground almonds. Pour the whole lot over the apricots and bake in the centre of the oven at 350°F, 180°C (Gas Mark 5) for 45 minutes. Serve hot with cream or ice cream.

Author's Note:
A really scrumptious dessert, and economical as well.

Patricia O'Leary

Production Assistant on 'Enlightenment' and 'The Two Doctors'

Patricia O'Leary joined the BBC after having been to stage school with Jamie (Frazer Hines) and deciding that acting was not for her (not Frazer's fault!). She learned all about television in the Sports Department, and then joined the Drama Department, for a 'quiet life' – something she is still looking for!

Pat has worked on many series and serials including *Softly, Softly*, *Sherlock Holmes*, *When the Boat Comes In*, *The Invisible Man*, and of course *Doctor Who*.

Camera Script Ice Cream

Ingredients:

Small carton of double (heavy) cream
Small carton of plain, unset yoghurt
3–4 pieces preserved ginger, finely chopped
2–3 tbs/2½–3¾ tbs/38–57 ml syrup from the ginger jar
Small pinch of salt

Method:
Whip double cream until very stiff. Add yoghurt and pinch of salt (salt is very important, otherwise it can separate). Beat slowly until well blended, adding ginger and syrup during the process. Freeze until mushy. Beat again slowly, then turn into serving dishes. Freeze until solid. Put into fridge 45 minutes before serving.

Author's Note:
This is really tasty, especially when served with hot ginger cake.

Sarah Sutton

Brandy Sponge Cake

Ingredients:

2 packets (approx. 24 fingers) sponge fingers
2 tbs/2½ tbs/38 ml brandy, to taste
1 tb/1¼ tb/30 g caster sugar
Coffee
Chocolate
1 pt/20 oz/6 dl whipped cream

Method:
Make up a *strong* cup of coffee, and add the caster sugar. Transfer this to a bowl and allow to cool. When the coffee is cool add the brandy. Dip each sponge finger in the coffee and place them side by side on a plate. After about eight, cover with a layer of cream. Repeat this twice. Place this in the fridge overnight. The next day cover the whole structure with the rest of the cream, including the sides and top the whole thing with grated chocolate. A calorie bomb – but delicious.

Author's Note:
I can guarantee that this is fantastic. Sarah served this cake at her 21st birthday party and it was a huge hit. Instead of using sponge fingers try using ginger snaps.

Johnny Byrne

Melkur Surprise

Ingredients:

1 tb/1¼ tb/19 ml honey
Thinly pared rind of 1 lemon
4 tbs/5 tbs/76 ml lemon juice
6 tbs/7½ tbs/114 ml white wine
2 tbs/2½ tbs/38 ml brandy
2 oz/56 g sugar
½ pt/10 oz/3 dl double (heavy) cream
Grated nutmeg
2 tbs/2½ tbs/60 g chopped toasted almonds

Method:
Put the lemon rind and juice and wine and brandy in a bowl and leave to infuse overnight.

Discard the lemon rind. Stir sugar into lemon mixture until dissolved, then stir in the cream. Beat until the mixture will hold a soft peak. Spoon into four glasses and sprinkle with a little grated nutmeg. Fold in toasted almonds, and serve.

Author's Note:
One more version of a syllabub for you to try and compare with the others in this book. Nyssa's favourite pudding.

John Leeson

K9

I first met John Leeson when I was working as an Assistant Floor Manager on *Underworld* and we have remained friends ever since.

John was marvellous during rehearsals. He would scuttle around on all fours pretending to be K9 and moving to where K9 would go in the studio. In fact, all John was obliged to do was stand and say the words, but because he is a true professional he acted out the role fully. This was fantastic for the director because they knew exactly where K9 would be.

Those of you who came to the *Doctor Who* celebrations at Longleat will remember K9, alias John Leeson, making all those very important announcements during the event.

Brown Bread Ice Cream

Ingredients:

½ pt/10oz/3 dl double (heavy) cream
1 oz/28 g vanilla sugar
3 oz/85 g stale wholemeal bread
3 oz/85 g soft brown sugar

Method:

Add the vanilla sugar to the cream, and whip it up until it becomes light and semi-stiff. Put into an ice tray in the freezer compartment of your refrigerator. As the mixture freezes, stir the sides into the middle.

Spread the breadcrumbs evenly over a non-stick or oiled baking tray, and sprinkle brown sugar over them evenly. Place the tray either under a grill or in a moderately hot oven until the sugar caramelises over the breadcrumbs. Stir from time to time. When the mixture is an even golden brown, allow it to cool completely and ensure that it is crumbly throughout.

When the ice cream is semi-hard, mix in the crumbs and refreeze for about two hours. A little brandy poured over each serving adds that final touch.

Author's Note:

This is a logical extension of the brown bread ice creams which were popular in England in the 18th and 19th centuries. It is absolutely delicious and another calorie buster. This is ideal for those languid summer dinner parties out on the terrace or patio, and a lovely bottle of Bollinger Special Cuvée or Krug 1976 served iced, of course, will really round off that lovely dinner party.

Terry Molloy

Davros's Extermination Pudding

Serves 4 people

Ingredients:

2 large bananas
2 egg whites
2 tbs/2½ tbs/60 g caster sugar
Raspberry jam (jelly)
Chopped nuts (of your choice)
Whipped cream

Method:
Pre-heat the oven to 325°F, 175°C (Gas Mark 3). Cut the bananas in their skins lengthwise and spread a layer of raspberry jam on the exposed side of the bananas. Then place the bananas with their skins on in an ovenproof dish (make sure that the skins are on the bottom side). Whip the egg whites (having separated them from the eggs beforehand) until the egg becomes white and stiff in fluffy firm peaks. Then carefully fold in the caster sugar. Spread the whites on top of the jam and sprinkle the chopped nuts over it.

Place in the oven and cook for 20 minutes, or until the egg whites are browned. Serve with a dollop of whipped cream. If you really want to be exterminated, a lovely portion of ice cream would be nice.

Author's Note:
I love baked or barbequed bananas. They remind me of the lovely barbeques that we have on those golden beaches in Australia where we wrap the bananas in tinfoil and throw them on the fire to cook in their skins. Delicious!

Davros has presented a delicious dessert, and he is determined to wreak his revenge on everyone by making you eat too much. After your third helping when you are relaxing in your chair, wishing that you had resisted the temptation, that is when he will strike. But who cares about the calories? If you've come this far, you might as well go the whole way. Eat your way to extermination!

Sarah Lee

Secretary to JNT

Sarah Lee is JNT's private secretary and the person who vets all of his telephone calls, visitors, and mail. To get to see or speak to JNT, one has to get past Sarah. She's also the daughter of Lynda Baron who played Captain Wrack in *Doctor Who*.

Sarah has concocted the 'Original Sarah Lee Gâteau' plus a cocktail of her own invention.

Before joining the BBC, Sarah gained 14 'O' Levels and 3 'A' Levels. She then worked in the theatre in many pantomimes and as an Assistant Stage Manager in three touring productions: *Not Now Darling*, *A Bed Full of Foreigners*, and *Key for Two*.

Her hobbies include horse riding, squash, keep-fit, music, cricket (as a spectator), and going out and having fun!

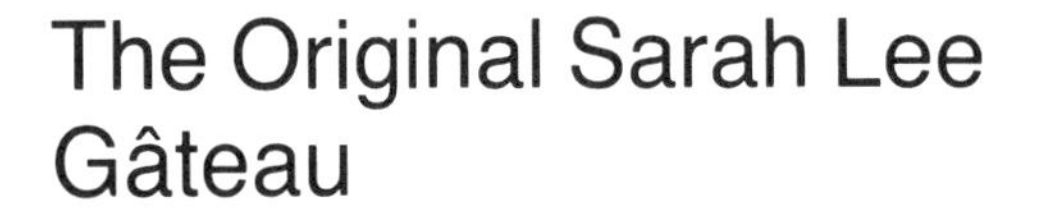

The Original Sarah Lee Gâteau

Ingredients:
Cake:

6 oz/171 g butter
6 oz/171 g sugar
3 eggs
1 oz/28 g cocoa powder
5 oz/143 g self-raising flour

Topping:
2 × 2 oz/56 g butter
Icing sugar
Cocoa powder
Chocolate buttons

Method:
Cream the butter and sugar. Add the eggs one at a time and then the cocoa powder. Fold in the flour. Bake for 20 minutes.

Topping:
Mix ½ butter and icing sugar with a little hot water until really smooth, add vanilla essence/cocoa powder.

To Decorate:
Spread the vanilla icing between the two halves of cake and the chocolate icing on top. Decorate with chocolate buttons.

Author's Note:
This is a lovely recipe from Sarah and tastes absolutely divine!

Caroline John

Doctor Elizabeth Shaw – companion to the third Doctor

Caroline John joined *Doctor Who* in 'Spearhead from Space', and then appeared in 'The Silurians', 'The Ambassadors of Death' and 'Inferno' when she left the series. All in all, she spent a year in the role as Liz Shaw. She then worked alongside Tom Baker in BBC TV's *The Hound of the Baskervilles*.

Caroline is married to actor Geoffrey Beevers, who played the part of the decaying Master in 'The Keeper of Traken', and she has chosen a delicious chocolate fudge cake as her recipe. She assures me that her children love it!

Chocolate Fudge Cake

Ingredients:

1½ cups plain flour
1½ cups sugar
4 oz/113 g lard, margarine or butter
2 large eggs
4 tbs/5 tbs/120 g chocolate powder
1 tsp/1¼ tsp/7.5 g bicarbonate of soda
1½ tsps/1¾ tsps/10 g cream of tartar
½ cup milk
½ cup boiling water

Method:
Use two bowls. Mix the sugar, eggs and butter in the first bowl, and mix the flour, chocolate powder and cream of tartar in the second. Then sieve the contents of the second bowl into the contents of the first bowl, and add ½ cup of milk gradually. When everything is mixed, beat well and add the boiling water. (Fear not, says Caroline, if it seems very liquidy.) Pour the mixture into a cake tin, lined with greased silver foil and put into an oven 350°–375°F, 180°–190°C (Gas Mark 4–5), for 45–60 minutes. Keep testing with a knitting needle to make sure that it is dry. Put the cake on a wire mesh and gradually peel off the silver foil while the cake is still hot so the steam can escape. When it is cold cut the cake horizontally in half and fill it with chocolate icing.

Chocolate Icing:
Ingredients:

3 oz/85 g butter
3 tbs/3¾ tbs/57 g chocolate powder
3 oz/85 g icing sugar

Method:
Sieve the chocolate powder and icing sugar together and blend with the butter until nice and smooth. This can be used for the top of the cake as well as the filling. There is another spread which can be used on top of the cake by using chocolate powder, icing sugar, and water.

Author's Note:
Chocolate cake has always been one of my favourites. The water-based icing is also good. Caroline thinks her choice of Chocolate Fudge Cake is very appropriate as she regards Liz Shaw as 'very sweet'!

Heather Hartnell

Chumblies

Ingredients:

4 oz/113 g butter or margarine
4 oz/113 g soft brown sugar
5 oz/143 g self-raising flour
2 eggs
1½ oz/45 g chopped glace cherries
1½ oz/45 g chopped walnuts
Little milk, if necessary

Method:
Blend the butter and sugar together till soft. Mix in the eggs, one by one, then the flour and fruit. Add a little milk if the mixture seems too soft. Put into bun cases, and bake for 15–20 minutes, at 375°F, 190°C (Gas Mark 5).

Author's Note:
This is one of my favourite recipes. I like it with as many cherries as possible and lots of custard.

When Bill Hartnell's grandchildren came to tea, Heather used to add a little icing on top of each cake, crowned with half a cherry or a walnut.

Carole Ann Ford

Susan – the Doctor's Granddaughter

In 1963 Carole Ann Ford was seen as the Doctor's granddaughter, Susan Foreman, a role that the fans were to remember fondly more than twenty years later.

The first story she appeared in was 'An Unearthly Child', and then followed 'The Daleks', The Edge of Destruction', 'Marco Polo', 'The Keys of Marinus', 'The Aztecs', 'The Sensorites', 'The Reign of Terror', 'Planet of Giants', and the story in which she left the series, 'The Dalek Invasion of Earth'.

She appeared in 10 stories and 51 episodes. This was in 1964, and when she left the show she appeared in *Whatever Happened to the Likely Lads?*

Illness and bringing up her daughter prevented Carole Ann from working until she recreated the role of Susan in 'The Five Doctors'. I am happy to say that offers of work are now pouring in for her. She still gets masses of fan mail for *Doctor Who* and always takes care to answer her fan letters herself.

Carole Ann is a very good cook and has given a dessert that is very popular with her own family.

Apple Thingy

Serves 4 hungry people

Ingredients:

1 large cooking apple per person
½ tb/10 ml honey per apple, according to taste
Small handful of sultanas
Sprinkling of flaked almonds
1½ oz/42 g butter
Powdered cinnamon
Powdered clove
Drambuie or Cointreau (optional)

Method:
Slice the apples thinly and place them in a deep pie dish. When the dish is half full sprinkle sultanas over the apples. Carry on filling the dish with the thinly sliced apples almost up to the top of the dish. Then sprinkle a teaspoon of cinnamon and cloves over the apples. Dot the top of the apples with butter and pour the honey over them. Place in an oven 350°–400°F, 180°–200°C (Gas Mark 4–6) for a couple of minutes till the butter has melted, then cover with an ovenproof plate. Cook for a further 30–45 minutes. When cooked, the apples should be really soft, almost fluffy. Sprinkle almonds on top and place the apples under a hot grill till they are brown. Serve with whipped cream and a dash (optional) of Drambuie or Cointreau. This could be served with a sponge finger or any suitable biscuit.

Author's Note:
I love baked apples, although until trying this recipe I had never eaten the apples with liqueur. Serve with sponge fingers. It can be also used as a base for a sponge mix for a heavier pudding. (If so, place the almonds on top).

Ian Marter

Harry Sullivan – Companion to the fourth Doctor

Ian Marter appeared in the following stories in *Doctor Who*: 'Robot', 'The Ark in Space', 'The Sontaran Experiment', 'Genesis of the Daleks', 'Revenge of the Cybermen', 'Terror of the Zygons' and 'The Android Invasion'.

Ian continued working as an actor after he left *Doctor Who*, and gradually became involved more and more in writing. I worked with Ian on a trilogy called *Elizabeth Alone* and we have been firm friends ever since.

Ian is married and has two sons who have appeared with him as his guests at various conventions in America. In the early 1980s he spent some time in New Zealand where he appeared in a highly successful TV series.

Ian has written several novelisations of *Doctor Who* stories for W.H. Allen's Target Books series.

Nautical Pudding

Although he was never seen at sea in the literal sense, Harry Sullivan did do his share of seafaring whenever he was not tripping over Aliens or getting in the Doctor's way. However he was capable of cooking only one dish. Fortunately it made use of ingredients fairly readily available aboard ship. So here is his recipe for Nautical Pudding.

Serves 4–6 hungry sailors

Ingredients:

6 oz/171 g brown flour
3 oz/85 g butter or margarine
2 oz/56 g brown sugar (the thick, dark sort)
12 oz/322 g dried prunes
1 orange
2 tbs/2½ tbs/38 ml rum (or more, according to taste)
Grated cheese
Water
Pinch of salt

Method:

Put the prunes into a saucepan and cover with water. Leave to soak overnight. Then simmer in the same water until soft and remove the stones. Add the rum, the juice of the orange and its rind chopped not too finely. Mix thoroughly and place in a pie dish.

Sift the flour and the salt, and make sure that they mix well. Rub the butter or margarine into the flour until the mixture atains the consistency of coarse breadcrumbs. Mix in the sugar and the grated cheese, if desired. Sprinkle the mixture over the prunes. Bake in the oven at 375–400°F, 190–200°C (Gas Mark 5–6), for about 20–25 minutes, until crisp. It is even better if it is slightly burnt.

This recipe is also quite effective against Cybermen and most Androids. Ian Marter loves it. For Landlubbers who may have such refinements to hand, it is even more startling when served with solid cold custard on top of the hot pudding and with cream and plain yoghurt poured generously over the whole creation.

Author's Note:

This pudding is obviously a pudding for health-conscious people, and having tried it, I recommend it.

George Baker

Login in 'Full Circle'

George Baker is an actor, writer and director. He was born on April 1, 1931 in Bulgaria, and was educated at Lancing College. George always wanted to act and after several jobs and National Service, he worked in about almost every repertory company in the country. He has appeared in plays in the West End of London and has done seasons with the Royal Shakespeare Company and the Old Vic, where he directed *The Lady's not for Burning*.

George has made over forty movies, some of his most famous being *The Dambusters*, *The Ship that Died of Shame*, *The Moonraker*, *A Hill in Korea*, *Goodbye Mr Chips*, *On Her Majesty's Secret Service*, *The Thirty-Nine Steps*, and *Hopscotch*. He has also starred in more than 100 TV plays and series including *Death of a Salesman*, *Medea*, *Candida*, *Rupert of Hentzau*, *I, Claudius* (he played the part of Tiberius) and more recently *Goodbye, Darling*, *Triangle*, and, of course, *Doctor Who*. George is the author of the award-winning play for TV, *The Fatal Spring*. He is married and has five daughters.

I first met George when he was appearing in *I, Claudius* for BBC TV and I was choreographing the series.

George is in great demand as an actor and as a writer. He is a wonderful cook and he has very kindly provided a delicious dessert recipe. It is terribly simple to make and not very expensive.

Decider's Dessert

Ingredients:

½ pt/10 oz/3 dl double (heavy) cream
1 tb/1 ¼ tb/30 g sugar
6 small macaroons
2 bananas
2 tsps/2½ tsps/12 ml lemon juice
1 tsp/1 ¼ tsp/6.2 ml brandy

Method:
Whip the sugar and the cream together. Then pound the macaroons to small pieces. Squash the bananas and add to the cream with the macaroons. Then add the lemon juice and brandy. Put into wine glasses and serve chilled.

Author's Note:
A decidedly lovely dessert for summer evenings, and I think that you will agree with me that this is a simple but effective recipe that will really impress your guests.

Dinah Sheridan

Chancellor Flavia's Favourite Syllabub

Ingredients:

½ pt/10 oz/3 dl double (heavy) cream
2–4 oz/56–113 g caster sugar
2 lemons
Small wine glass of brandy

Method:
Beat together the cream and the grated rind of one lemon. As the mixture thickens add the juice of both lemons and the sugar. Adjust the amount to suit your taste. Beat until it holds its shape. Flavour with the brandy, or sherry if preferred.

Serve in small glasses or pots. Chill for an hour.

Author's Note:
Absolutely delicious. I sometimes add stem ginger, to the syllabub or even raspberries (in which case I use raspberry liqueur rather than brandy).

Nicholas Courtney

Coupe Nick

Serves 6–8 people

Ingredients:

½ pt/275 ml double (heavy) cream
1 lemon
4 oz/113 g sugar
3 fl oz/85 ml cider

Method:
Put the cream into a bowl and whip until thick. Add the finely grated rind of the lemon and the strained juice with the sugar. Gradually blend in the cider. Chill until needed, then spoon into individual serving dishes.

Author's Note:
A variation of Chancellor Flavia's Syllabub, this time using cider. It is delicious with sweet biscuits.

Dick Mills

Pavlova Perfection

Ingredients:

3 large egg whites
6 oz/171 g caster sugar
½ pt/10 oz/3 dl whipped cream
12 oz/341 g soft fruit (raspberries, strawberries)
Little icing sugar

Method:
Pre-heat the oven to 300°F, 150°C (Gas Mark 2).

Place the egg whites in a large clean bowl. Whisk until they form soft peaks and you can turn the bowl upside down without them sliding out.

Whisk the sugar into the egg whites 1 oz at a time. Take a metal tablespoon and spoon the meringue mixture on to a lightly oiled baking sheet, lined with lightly oiled greaseproof paper. Form the mixture into a circle of about 8 inches diameter. Make a round depression in the centre and, using a skewer, make little swirls in the meringue all around the edge, lifting the skewer to make peaks.

Place the baking sheet in the oven and immediately turn down the heat to 275°F, 140°C (Gas Mark 1) and leave to cook for 1 hour.

After 1 hour, turn the heat right off, but leave the Pavlova inside the oven until completely cold. (It is best to make a Pavlova in the evening and leave overnight to dry out.)

To serve the Pavlova, lift it from the baking sheet, peel off the paper and place in a serving dish. Just before serving, spread the cream on top, arrange the fruit on top of the cream and dust with a little sifted icing sugar.

Author's Note:
Being half-Australian I love this dessert. You can use any fruit of your choice with the Pavlova: mandarins or bananas are an interesting choice.

Sarah Hellings

Winter Fruit Salad

Ingredients:

2 tins *white* peaches (from a good delicatessen)
4 large bananas, not too ripe
6 tbs/7½ tbs/114 ml dark rum
3 tbs/3¾ tbs/90 g light soft brown sugar
1 oz/28 g butter

Method:
Chop the fruit into large bite-size pieces. Put into an ovenproof casserole with half the juice, the rum and the sugar. Dot the top with flakes of butter. Place in the top of a very hot oven and eat your main course. Serve very hot with very cold thick double cream.

Author's Note:
In this dish, pears can be substituted for peaches, and a tin of apricots can be added to make it go even further. This is a very simple and economic dessert and is truly mouth-watering. And who cares about the calories? Eat and enjoy!

DRINKS

Peter Davison

The fifth Doctor

Peter trained at the Central School of Speech and Drama and spent a year at the Nottingham Playhouse, followed by a spell at the Young Lyceum Company. His first television appearance was in the Independent TV series *The Tomorrow People*. He then followed this by playing Tom Holland in H. E. Bates's *Love For Lydia*.

He had a great personal success as Tristan Farnon in the highly popular TV series *All Creatures Great and Small*, and has also appeared in the two situation comedies, *Holding the Fort* and *Sink or Swim*. In March 1982 he was the subject of Thames Television's *This Is Your Life*.

Peter has presented *'L' Driver*, a programme for foreigners taking their British driving test, and has also done a major British tour of *Barefoot in the Park*, in which he worked with his wife, Sandra Dickinson.

The Doctor's Chocolate Malted Medicine

Serves 1 Doctor or 2 companions!

Ingredients:

4 heaped tsps/5 tsps/30 g cocoa
2 heaped tsps/2½ tsps/15 g Horlicks
500 ml dairy ice cream
½ pt/10 oz/3 dl milk
2 squirts of chocolate syrup

Method:

Put the cocoa and Horlicks into a cup. Add a drip of water and mix to a paste.

Take one common-or-garden intergalactic kitchen blender and empty the ice cream and milk into it. Blend for a parsec and then add the cocoa paste and the chocolate syrup. Blend again until full integration is complete.

Author's Note:

Once again, I have to confess to a passion for this recipe. Try putting a few ice cubes into it as well – that will really put your teeth on edge.

Nicola Bryant

Perpugilliam's Purple Punch

Serves approximately 20 people

Ingredients:

2½ × 1 pint 7 fl oz (750 ml) bottles of chilled Ginger Ale
3 × 75 cl bottles of young chilled Claret
Ice cubes
2 limes

Method:
Fill punch bowl with ice cubes; pour claret and ginger ale over ice cubes; slice limes and float on top of punch.

Author's Note:
Mmmmmm!

Nicola's Nectarine Cup

Serves 15 people

Ingredients:

2 × 75 cl bottles dry champagne or dry sparkling white wine
3 fl oz/½ cup/75 ml curacao
3 fl oz/½ cup/75 ml brandy
1 fl oz/13¼ tbs/25 ml lemon juice
5 tsps/6¼ tsps/37 g icing sugar
1¼ pt/7½ dl soda water
3 sliced nectarines
6 oz/225 g raspberries
Sprig of mint
Ice cubes

Method:
Stand punch bowl in a large bowl filled with crushed ice. Mix liquid ingredients together, adding soda water last. Stir in sugar. Take care as it's very effervescent. Add sliced nectarines and raspberries. Garnish with mint and serve immediately.

Author's Note:
A delicious punch from a delicious girl!

Cyril Luckham

White Guardian's Wine Cup

Makes approximately 6½ pints

Ingredients:

Crushed ice
3 bottles white wine
¾ bottle dry sherry
4 tbs/5 tbs/95 ml curacao
4 splits tonic water
3 slices cucumber
Slice of apple
Sprig of borage

Method:
Mix all the ingredients together in one or more jugs and chill before serving.

Author's Note:
Refreshing but deceptively rosey on the palate.

Fiona Cumming

Enlightenment Lemonade

Serves 6 people

Ingredients:

12 lemons
2 lb/906 g sugar
½ pt/10 oz/3 dl water
1 tsp/1¼ tsp/7.5 g tartaric acid

Method:
Grate the lemon rind and extract the juice. Boil them together. Bring the sugar and water to the boil *very* slowly, so that the sugar melts before the liquid boils.

Add the lemon liquid and bring the sugar and lemons to the boil once more, and then add the tartaric acid.

Let the lemonade cool, then bottle and keep in fridge. Dilute with cold water to taste.

Author's Note:
Enlightenment Lemonade is a recipe of Fiona's great-aunt, Mabel Holland. Cheers!

Sarah Lee

Sonic Screwdriver

Ingredients:

Ice
Mint
2 shots Vodka
2 shots Martini
4 shots orange juice

Method:
Mix all the ingredients in a cocktail shaker. Serve 'shaken but not stirred'.

Author's Note:
A wonderful cocktail – handle with care!

John Nathan-Turner

'No Comment' Nectar

Serves 6 people

Ingredients:

2 squares chocolate
¼ pt/5 oz/1½ dl black coffee
4 oz/113 g sugar
2 small cinnamon sticks
2 blades of mace
4 cloves
1 tsp/1¼ tsp/7.5 g nutmeg
½ pt/10 oz/3 dl milk infused with spices for 30 minutes
Whipped cream

Method:
Heat the chocolate with the coffee until melted. Stir in the sugar and milk and allow to cool for five minutes. Serve topped with cream.

THE BRIGADIER'S BANQUET

Nick has decided that if he were to throw a dinner party and invited you, this is the menu he would serve you.

All the dishes are his personal favourites. Here then is a typical 'Brig' Menu.

MENU

BORSCHT AU BRIG CHER

* * *

SAUMON FUMÉ ÉSCOSSAIS (STEWART CLAN)

* * *

LE FILET DE BOEUF DIANE (FEMME DU BRIG)

* * *

LÉGUMES DE LA SAISON (PRINTEMPS)

* * *

COUPE NICK (SORBET)

* * *

CAFÉ GRECQUE

* * *

VIN ROSÉ DE CALIFORNIE (CONVENTION LOCATION SAN JOSE)

* * *

CHOCOLATS (APRÈS HUIT)

* * * * * * * *

INDEX